D0776707

"Gail Steinel and M..... hat' business leaders with priceless experiences and insights. *Excuse Me, Aren't You In Charge?* not only gives the reader those priceless gems, but also does so in an inspiring and entertaining package. This is a book that will make you think and laugh at the same time. Every experienced leader will delight in seeing their own lives reflected in the anecdotes that Gail and Mike have woven into this fascinating read. It inspired me to reach out to the people who work with me, challenge them to be better leaders, and move my organization forward with renewed enthusiasm. Both Gail and Mike are especially adept crisis leaders, and their time in the crucibles of critical incidents is particularly noteworthy and evident throughout the pages of their book. *Excuse Me* is a particularly valuable read for MBA students and aspiring leader-managers because it offers what can't be taught—the lessons of experience."

—Col. Thomas A. Kolditz, PhD, author, *In Extremis Leadership: Leading as if Your Life Depended on It;* professor, West Point

"The most important lessons in life are learned from stories. Mike Policano and Gail Steinel have collected a great set of stories for managers. Some you may ignore after reading them, but others will stay with you and be useful for a long time. Read them all—pick the ones you like and share them with your friends."

—Paul W. Marshall, professor of business management practice at Harvard Business School

"*Excuse Me, Aren't You In Charge?* is an array of interesting and enjoyable stories, laced with plenty of lessons learned as well as good common sense. Even the most capable and experienced of business leaders will learn some new moves."

—Antonio Alvarez III, managing director, Alvarez & Marsal's European Division

"I couldn't help but smile as I read Gail and Mike's storytelling on a recent cross-country flight. It's just amazing how many long-forgotten experiences in my own business life were triggered by this book. *Excuse Me, Aren't You In Charge?* is fast, light reading that puts perspective on everyday management. Bravo!"

—Don Wood, president and CEO, Federal Realty Investment Trust

"Highly successful companies thrive on clear strategic decision making and great leadership. Gail Steinel and Mike Policano have assembled a delightful compilation of their experiences that not only provide great insights to strategic leadership but also provide highly enjoyable reading. Read this book—you will laugh and learn—a great combination."

—Andrew J. Policano, Dean, The Paul Merage School of Business

"This book captures what's missing in so many leadership books—stories. In an age of excessive theory regarding leadership, readers will enjoy practical examples of how leaders lead through a series of short, punchy, entertaining stories."

—Bob O'Shea, co-CEO, Silver Point Capital

"Sadly, leading through adversity has now become a core required executive competency across all industries. This book is delightfully free of the distorting personal aggrandizement or simplistic textbook checklists which are the too common choices on the bookshelf of related titles. In addition to the powerful lessons, the reader is treated to fascinating sagas of leadership."

—Jeffrey Sonnenfeld, senior associate dean, Yale School of Management; author, *Firing Back: How Great Leaders Rebound after Career Disasters*

Excuse Me, Aren't You In Charge?

+ +

INSIGHTFUL SNIPPETS TO RECHARGE YOUR LEADERSHIP BATTERIES

+ +

Gail Steinel & Mike Policano

EMERALD
BOOK CO.

The net profits from the sale of this book will be donated to charity.

Published by Emerald Book Company
4425 S. Mo Pac Expressway, Suite 600
Austin, TX 78735
www.emeraldbookcompany.com

Distributed by Emerald Book Company
For ordering information or special discounts for bulk purchases, please contact
Emerald Book Company at 4425 S. Mo Pac Expressway,
Suite 600, Austin, TX 78735, (512) 891-6100.

Design and composition by Greenleaf Book Group LLC
Cover design by Greenleaf Book Group LLC

Publisher's Cataloging-In-Publication Data
(Prepared by The Donohue Group, Inc.)

Steinel, Gail.
   Excuse me, aren't you in charge? : insightful snippets to recharge your leadership batteries / Gail Steinel & Mike Policano. -- 1st ed.

   p. ; cm.

   ISBN-13: 978-1-934572-11-5
   ISBN-10: 1-934572-11-X

1. Leadership. 2. Executive ability. 3. Crestive ability in business. I. Policano,
Mike. II. Title.

HD57.7 .S734 2008
658.4/09   2008907263

Printed in the United States of America on acid-free paper
08 09 10 11 12 13 14   10 9 8 7 6 5 4 3 2 1
First Edition

CONTENTS

+ +

READER BEWARE

+ +

We are storytellers. What we have done in this book is collect some of our favorite stories—all of which are true, except for the ones that are not.

Although leadership is the theme common to most of the stories, you'll notice that they're not in any particular order. Neither do we cover all possible topics. Some people who read the early manuscript asked Gail, "Why don't you say anything about women in business?" They asked Mike, "What about all your sales and marketing stories?" What we told these well-meaning people is that no, those stories are not in this book. Maybe they will be in the next one.

We were also asked why we had decided to write a book together. To understand that, we need to go back a bit. For nearly three decades, Mike has provided restructuring advisory services to the financial workout and bankruptcy community. Gail has spent her professional life in the global consulting industry. But thirty years ago they were just starting their careers. Mike had been at Arthur Andersen for two years when Gail showed up for an interview. Mike and another junior associate were picked to take her to lunch. The way Gail remembers it, during the course of the meal it came out that Mike was the president of the office's Thursday Night Drinking Club. Once Gail heard this she knew this was the firm for her. Funny, she drinks only Diet Cokes now.

Mike has a different recollection: "My colleague asked Gail to tell us about herself, and three hours later, Gail finally stopped for breath. It was the world's longest one-hour lunch, and I got in trouble for it."

Mike persuaded Gail to start speaking at MBA programs with him in 2003. Gail noticed that many speakers had a book. Mike said, "So, let's write a book."

Gail replied, "Mike, I don't write. I talk."

He replied, "No worries. Just talk out loud and type as you speak."

We titled this book *Excuse Me, Aren't You in Charge? Insightful Snippets to Recharge Your Leadership Batteries* because we believe that leadership qualities go beyond having the right degrees or years of experience. We believe each story has some unique insight to offer beyond conventional business wisdom, and we hope this book will help you identify and nurture the potential leaders you meet in your professional and personal lives.

We think telling stories is an effective way of sharing our unique insights and approaches to various situations. We are not aware of anyone who agrees with us.

We would love your input. You can e-mail us at excusemeleaders@gmail.com.

We are donating all of the net profits from this book to charitable and educational organizations. At least some good will come from our literary efforts. So, here are the stories that we present for your enjoyment, reflection, and use.

YOUR FEES ARE VERY HIGH

+ +

Several years ago two of my partners sold an advisory engagement to a publicly held manufacturing company headquartered just outside of Washington, D.C. The company's bank lenders were very unhappy with its performance, and we were hired to help the manufacturer come up with a new strategy and business plan.

I was in Bermuda on vacation at the time, but when I got back we decided that I would be the partner on the job. I chose Walt, a recent hire whom I had just met, to work with me. The morning Walt and I visited the company, we introduced ourselves to Ben, the CEO, and John, the CFO, and went over the scope of the engagement. Ben was a big guy, a former Marine colonel with an imposing presence. We took a break for lunch, agreeing to settle the exact financial arrangements in the afternoon. Around 2:00 p.m., Walt, Ben, John, and I reconvened in the conference room.

I started the conversation by asking Ben if he had any questions or comments about our engagement letter.

"Yes, I do," Ben said bluntly. "Your fees are very high."

I looked down at a copy of our engagement letter and counted silently to myself—one thousand one, one thousand two, one thousand three—before continuing. It was a long silence, especially for a meeting of that kind.

Finally, I looked up at Ben and said, "Actually, our fees are *outrageously* high."

There was another beat of silence, and then Ben chuckled.

I continued, "It's hard to argue with someone who agrees with you, isn't it?"

Ben laughed again and said, "Yeah, it really is."

"Any other comments?" I asked.

Realizing I had just settled the issue of our hourly rates, Ben then asked, "Is your retainer negotiable?"

"Absolutely," I replied. "We can negotiate as much as you want."

Ben looked at me sharply and cocked his head. "Are you *willing* to change the amount?"

"Absolutely not," I replied.

"Give me the piece of paper." Ben signed it and walked out.

John was stunned. "I can't believe that just happened."

"Actually, John, he didn't have a chance," I said. "First, I don't discount our fees. Second, it is golf season. I especially wouldn't discount our fees during golf season. I would golf instead."

John shook his head, "Before lunch, Ben had said to me, 'Watch how I get them to cut their fees.' But the next thing I knew, the agreement was signed and the meeting over."

Later that night at dinner, Walt asked, "Hey, Mike, have you ever used that line about your fees before?"

"No," I said, and raised my glass. "It worked pretty well didn't it?"

Walt replied, "I have to tell you, I was worried. As you know, I joined your firm without meeting you. When I heard you say that our rates were outrageous, I thought, *Can I get my old job back?* But then it was a done deal. You hadn't budged an inch. What made you say that?"

"Walt, I looked at our letter and thought, *Our fees really are high.* Then I looked at Ben and wondered what I could possibly tell him that would convince him the fees were not high. Absolutely nothing. So I agreed with him."

"But why do you think Ben gave in so quickly?" Walt asked.

"Simple. He saw in my eyes that I was not going to discount our fees. He knew it was pointless to try."

"How did you convince him of that? You hardly said anything."

"The key to creating leverage in any negotiation is demonstrating that you can accept losing. In other words, I would have been perfectly happy to lose the engagement and go home. My body language told him that. I was not going to give in, and he saw that. He's a smart guy. He accepted reality. That's how it works, Walt."

SCREWED THE WORST

+ +

I accepted a position within my firm to take over leadership of one of its largest business groups on a Friday. One hundred executives from that group had already been invited to attend a meeting the following Monday in Las Vegas. So my first task in my new role was to brief this group on the change in management, and what it would mean for them.

The day after my promotion, I flew to Las Vegas to prepare for the meeting. I knew there were going to be some challenges in leading this group. Revenues had been declining for a number of years. To try and remedy that, previous management had fired a number of junior people, but now the group was top-heavy, and the cost per hour was too high. At this point, profitability was sinking even faster than revenues. However, I was still excited about my new position because I felt all these problems were fixable, and I intended to work with the team to fix them.

It was therefore a shock on Saturday when I began to meet the members of the team who, like me, had shown up early at the hotel. I had thought we'd have a problem with low morale. I hadn't expected the anger.

"No offense, Gail," one woman told me, "but a new leader just means they're rearranging the deck chairs on the *Titanic.*"

"I'm leaving at the first opportunity," a man said. "This group cannot be saved."

Because the group had been put together through acquisitions, it was now composed of a number of different factions, none of which trusted any of the others. People had stories to tell of promises that were not kept, compensation expectations that were not met, and promotions that never materialized.

"No one has listened. No one has appreciated what we've been through the past few years," one senior manager told me.

I had already prepared my presentation with its messages and plans and statements of direction, but I saw that it clearly wouldn't fly. These managers were in no mood to listen to such things. And because they were so focused on past wrongs, they would not be able to focus on the future.

On Monday, when I took the stage, I faced a sea of angry faces and folded arms that said plainer than words, "Here comes more BS from management." I had thought hard about the situation all Saturday and Sunday. So instead of giving my carefully prepared opening presentation, I made an announcement.

"There's a lot of baggage from the past weighing down all of us in this room," I said.

The room was suddenly quiet.

"How many people in this room think they have been screwed?" I asked.

There was some scattered laughter. The atmosphere noticeably lightened.

"Seriously," I said, "I want to see a show of hands."

Almost everyone in the room raised a hand. Now there was more laughter.

"We are going to have a contest. Everyone will tell his or her story. The winner of this contest is the person that we all agree has been screwed the worst. I will give a bonus to the winner. He or she will have earned it."

The reaction in the room was more laughter and an increasing sense of excitement for the contest.

So we started the contest. I asked for volunteers. Slowly at first, but then more eagerly, people came up on stage to tell their tales of woe. The stories were truly amazing.

One guy told us that he had announced he was leaving the company but his boss had talked him out of it by promising him a raise and a promotion. The man called his prospective employer and said he had changed his mind. But that very day, his boss was fired. His replacement refused to honor the verbal commitment. The employee was left stuck in the same dead-end job, with no prospect of a raise or promotion, and no new opportunity to pursue.

Another man had moved his family to Europe at the request of the company. When it was time to transfer back, a new manager would not honor a promise to relocate him back in his home state. Although the man eventually made it back to the United States, he was demoted and lost his title and level of pay.

We heard many similar stories that day. But instead of anger, a sense of camaraderie started to grow among the people in the room. We began to have fun.

The winner was a guy who had joined a company as a partner in 2001. When he arrived on board, he signed a promissory note to a bank to pay for his capital contribution. Even though his company was acquired by ours a few months later, he still had to repay that note. To make matters worse, when the company he was with was absorbed into our company, his compensation was reduced because he had not had enough time as a partner to build his book of business. He was still paying his note payments each month and had not had a raise in three years.

We all applauded him.

Once I was back onstage, I said, "We have a clear winner. He has been screwed the worst. We all agree he deserves the bonus payment."

The audience laughed. There were even some cheers.

"By definition, if he is the worst case, then the rest of us are better off than he is. If we agree that there are people worse off than we are, can we let go of the past and all its baggage?" I looked around the hall and saw people nodding, and I felt we'd accomplished something important.

After the break, I was able to give the planned presentation about the future. The entire tone of the meeting had changed.

Not only did the guy get his "screwed the worst" bonus, but we also eventually went through a compensation review and fixed his and several others' problems. Most importantly, we all began the turnaround of the business together.

Sometimes you have to try something new to get the tone you need.

WHY ISN'T SHE
LISTENING TO ME?

+ +

I had a meeting scheduled with a top executive at one of my clients. However, it quickly became apparent to me that she was not focused and was not listening as intently as usual, so I asked her if there was something on her mind.

"Yes, Gail, as a matter of fact there is. I just left a meeting with the CEO. He asked me to lead a major cost-reduction initiative. His goal is to cut $300 million in costs. He wants a rough plan by next week."

"That's great. What's the issue?" I asked.

She said, "I don't think I can meet that deadline. My team is flat out on priority projects. They don't have any more bandwidth."

It was clear that this was now the number one thing on her mind, and she was not going to be able to focus on our agenda. When I suggested we scrap our agenda and instead draft a plan for her new initiative right then, she eagerly agreed. By the end of the meeting, we had a rough draft of a plan, which we refined over the next week.

A few days later, Mina called to tell me that the CEO of the company where she worked had green-lighted the project. I congratulated her and wished her luck with the initiative.

Mina said, "Well, he also approved the hiring of consultants. I want to work with you and your firm, so let's get started."

Sensing the situation resulted in lucrative business. Focus on the other person's needs instead of your own agenda.

YOU CAN'T WIN THIS

+ +

Jeff, a former partner, and I were meeting with Marvin, the owner of an apparel company, to finalize our engagement letter.

Marvin said, "Mike, I want to negotiate your fees."

"I'm sorry, Marvin. I can't do that."

"What do you mean you can't do that?"

"Marvin, I can't negotiate with you because you can't win."

"What do you mean I can't win? I'm a good negotiator."

"Marvin, I'm sure you are a good negotiator. But you can't win."

Marvin began to get angry, and I could sense that Jeff was wondering what I was doing.

Marvin almost shouted, "I can absolutely win!"

"No, Marvin, I can't let you win, and here is why. Why are you hiring me?"

Marvin replied, "I am hiring you because I need you to negotiate with the banks."

"Exactly. Now, if I couldn't negotiate my own fees, then you would wonder how I could negotiate with the banks. So you see, I can't let you win. Now, just sign the letter."

Marvin signed the letter.

On the way back to our office, Jeff said, "Mike, where in the world did you come up with that crazy negotiating strategy?"

"To tell you the truth, I just made it up."

CHEAP IS EXPENSIVE

+ +

Having been in the consulting business most of my working life, I'm used to selling services rather than buying them.

When Andersen was being dismantled, the board approved pursuing an opportunity to sell the entire global consulting group. This involved operations in eighty-five countries and was an extremely complex transaction, so I called Mike, who is an expert in troubled companies.

"Mike, I'm sure you've seen the news. I need your help."

He said, "Sure, as soon as I get back from my golf outing in Hilton Head, I'll be happy to help."

"Mike, this is a crisis involving the jobs of ten thousand people. Can't the golf wait? I need you now."

He left that day for New York, which tells you how serious the situation was.

When he arrived, the first thing he did was start a list of all the experts we needed to hire—lawyers, investment bankers, etc.

I said, "Mike, do you know how hard it was to get the company to approve hiring you? We already have more lawyers then anyone will ever need."

"Gail, this is going to be extremely complex, and we must have a very well-run process. We need experts in each of these disciplines," replied Mike.

"Okay, then you hire them," I said. "I don't have the time to pull this together."

"No, you must interview them and be comfortable with whomever you hire."

So I found the time to set up meetings and interview several investment banking firms and hire a lead firm to represent the group.

Mike then said, "Great, now we need to hire attorneys."

"You do it, I have no time."

Mike said, "You have to interview them and be comfortable."

So I held interviews and hired a law firm.

Mike said, "Great, now we need to hire a compensation consulting firm."

"No. I have no time and that would never get approved."

When the transaction was completed, I finally had some free time. I used it to reflect and realized I had learned the following lessons:

- You need experts.
- You need experts you like.
- You need the right team.
- You cannot be cheap because cheap is expensive. It is easy to focus on cost. But when you are in a crisis, you have no time for rework. You need the best experts available.

By the way, we should have hired the compensation experts.

TRUST IS LIKE A
BANK ACCOUNT

+ +

In order to expect trust from your employees in a crisis, you have to build up credibility and trust before the crisis occurs. It is like making deposits in an account during normal times—a trust account—so that you can make withdrawals during a crisis.

In 2002, I was the head of the Global Business Consulting Group of Arthur Andersen when the firm was indicted by the Justice Department. A process was started to dismantle the firm. For the audit and tax practices, the process was on a country-by-country basis. Each country determined which of the four accounting firms it would sell the business to. In the United States, individuals or groups of partners and their teams went to different firms.

At that time, the accounting firms were divesting their consulting businesses and were therefore not potential buyers for the consulting business. The consulting business was also run on a more national and global basis than the other practices within the firm. Globally, the consulting business had about $2.5 billion in revenue, with ten thousand employees in more than 175 offices in eighty-five countries. As the global managing partner running the consulting business, I believed that I was responsible for finding new successful careers for all ten thousand employees while maximizing value to Andersen.

This was a time of very high anxiety and distrust. People were concerned about their ability to earn a living and to take care of their families and other obligations.

Fortunately, during my twenty-three-year tenure at the firm, my leadership team and I had earned a reputation for talking straight and honoring our commitments. We would not have made it through this crisis without that existing reputation.

The day I learned of the indictment, I sent out the following voice mail message to all our business consulting employees: "Okay guys, this is Gail. You all know what is going on. I am sure your mother, your father, and your significant other are saying to you, 'Leave this place and go get a new job.' The reason I know this is because my mother is saying that to me.

"But I am going to ask you to do me a favor. I am going to ask you not to leave yet. We have all had discussions about this. We think we are worth more together than apart. We think that each one of you can be more successful if you start in a new firm with the same team you have worked with for years. In addition, we have support staff to consider. The people who work in the mailroom and elsewhere will have a better chance for a new job if they go with you, the consultants, on their team.

"So, what I am going to ask you to do is to hold together for a while. It's not going to be easy. Give us a little bit of time to try to see if we can make a transaction for the entire global business.

"I have no idea if we can do this. I have never done this before in my life. I don't know if it is saleable. And, oh, by the way, most people tell us it is not.

"What I will promise is to send a voice mail update every week and let you know where we stand. If I conclude that this cannot be done, I will let you know. Since your leadership team and I will have meetings with the top executives of all the potential acquirers, we will enhance your marketability during this process by telling them more about this successful business that you have all built. I need you to stick together, which I know will not be easy with all the uncertainty that exists right now."

Before I sent out the voice mail, every communications expert I talked to had warned me that the message left too many unanswered questions, that the employees would expect more answers.

I said, "I don't have the answers. These are very smart and capable people, and right now they are anxious and skeptical. If ever there was a moment that called for complete honesty, this is it. I am going to bank on the trust that the consulting leadership team has built up over the years."

We tried to continue to earn that trust during the crisis. We never promised them anything we could not deliver. Although dates did slip during the three and a half months it took to complete a transaction and there were many disappointments, I sent a new voice mail every week with whatever new information we had.

The trust, respect, and loyalty existed at every level within the consulting business. It was built upon a strong culture within all of Andersen. The most inexperienced consultants trusted their managers, who trusted their senior managers, who trusted their partners, who trusted the leaders of that group, who trusted their regional leaders, who trusted me. We were all in it together.

We had made deposits and earned their trust during good times.

When the crisis occurred, and we desperately needed the trust, the account was full.

Most of the group did stay together and was part of a set of complex transactions with one buyer. The transition was very difficult and complicated by the post–9/11 decline in consulting revenue. Many people left the company that bought the business and ironically ended up at one of the four global accounting firms. Unfortunately, at the time of the crisis, those firms were not an option for all of the consultants due to the public perception—which has since changed—that they should not have consulting businesses. But at least it was a soft landing that allowed everyone the chance to choose their future career moves. To this day, I meet people who tell me that every week they listened to the voice mails with their significant other because they believed what they heard, even when they did not like what they heard.

FILL PEOPLE'S CUPS
WITH ENERGY

+ +

Have you ever worked with someone who often left you energized after you were with them? Someone who gave you that I-can-do-anything feeling? If you have, then you know you have been in contact with a true leader.

I believe that one of the key roles of leaders is to fill their team with energy. The most highly talented team will not perform well if it is running on empty. And it's easy for leaders themselves to run out of energy as they constantly handle problems and difficult situations. Therefore, leaders need to be able to refill their energy cups as well as the cups of their teams when they are running low.

I often discuss the concept of filling energy cups with my teams. About half of them initially think I am crazy. One person who thought this way was Fernando, one of my direct reports. A very aggressive, hardworking, and action-oriented individual, Fernando considered my concept of filling energy cups to be nothing but happy talk. He said he wanted to focus on getting results.

"Do I usually get results?" I asked him.

"Well, yes," he replied, thoughtfully.

"Can you think of any instances in which you called me and your cup was empty?"

Fernando thought for a moment, and then said, "Well, once I called you regarding a major client who had significant cost overruns. We were having trouble getting the client to stick to the original scope. We had a poorly written contract that allowed for too much interpretation about what was included in the original scope. The client kept adding new things but would not approve change orders.

"Although I tried to fix the situation, it was not working. I knew this situation was only going to get worse. I was really frustrated and stressed about it."

When I asked him what happened, he replied, "You called one day and asked how I was doing. Although I said I was okay, you said you weren't convinced and pressed me to tell you what was on my mind. I started to tell you about this client but stopped and said I didn't want to bother you. You told me that I wasn't bothering you and that a leader's job was to help teams be better at their jobs. We then started to brainstorm about how we could fix the client relationship. You made some suggestions that were helpful, and you picked out my best idea and made a big deal of it."

"What was that idea?"

"I said I was going to review with the client what they had asked for in our first meeting and remind them why we had structured the project the way we did."

"That was a great idea!" I said. "Since they'd strayed so much from their original goals, it was right to remind them of how it all got started."

"That's exactly what you said back then, Gail."

"Then what happened?" I asked.

"You told me I was great at solving client problems and offered to hold another brainstorming session after I had some time to reflect on the discussion with the client."

"How did that talk fill your energy cup?"

He answered, "Well, for starters, you validated that it was a big issue and not an easy one to solve. You helped to reinforce my confidence, which was beginning to fail me. The conversation broke my mental block and allowed the ideas to start flowing for me again. Sharing some of your prior experience and ideas helped me to think of new approaches to try with the client.

"The bottom line is that you helped stop my negative spiral and got me to start believing in myself again. You gave me back a positive I-can-do-it attitude."

Fernando finished by saying, "Okay, I get it. So there is more to this energy cup thing than happy talk."

DRAINING THE ENERGY CUP

+ +

If filling people's energy cups is powerful and has a positive impact, draining their energy cups is twice as powerful but, unfortunately, has a negative impact.

Marion, a direct report, and her entire team had worked for months on a very complex client opportunity. We had solved many issues, but we had come across a particularly complicated and financially risky contract. Finally, the time came for us to hold the corporate deal review call and to perform an independent review of the deal to assess the relative financial risks and rewards.

At the start of the call, we summarized our opportunity and our plans to mitigate the risks for the review committee. When the call ended, I had a separate meeting with the team. They were down and demoralized.

One team member asked, "Gail, why are we killing ourselves to get this deal done? The review committee didn't even seem to care. Never once did anyone on that call act excited about the business."

I replied, "The deal was approved. We only have this one open issue, and it will happen."

There was silence.

"You know, you're right, but why doesn't it feel good?" asked one member of the team.

"Because John zapped our energy buckets," said Marion. It was true. John's unenthusiastic attitude over the phone had demoralized our team.

When I ran into John a few days later I asked him why he had acted the way he had on the call.

"The team had the rest of the deal covered, so there was no need to comment on it," he answered.

"But you never said any of that."

John was surprised. "Did they need to hear me say it?"

"Yes!"

Unfortunately, John never understood this conversation. I suspect he is still draining people's energy cups. Take a moment and reflect on these last two stories. I know you can think of some people who filled your energy cup and others who drained it. For which person did you work harder and produce more? You can choose which type of leader you will be.

LET PEOPLE FOLLOW
THEIR PASSIONS

+ +

One day a woman who was a first-year staff person in my group came to see me.

"Ellen, what's up?" I asked her.

"I have noticed that we don't have many African-Americans in our practice."

Before she could continue, I started my very politically correct response explaining our diversity efforts.

Ellen listened attentively, but my answer didn't alleviate her concern. "I think we need to expand the sources we pursue for candidates."

"Ellen, let me explain how we select our sources." I then gave her all the data and explained to her in depth how we selected our sources.

After a lengthy discussion, Ellen said, "I'm not here to complain, Gail. I have some ideas and would like to lead an effort to see if we can make improvements."

"Well, what are your ideas?"

This was the moment when her eyes lit up and she began to detail a well-thought-out plan. She wanted to work with a professional society of African-American engineers to which she belonged. She had identified schools with a high percentage of African-American students. She also had many other ideas.

When I asked her what she would need to activate her plan, she bounced out of her chair and went to the whiteboard. It was so much fun to watch her excitement and animation.

I said, "But Ellen, we have a recruiting department and this is their job. They already have several diversity initiatives under way. Plus, you have a full client load to manage."

Her reply surprised me. "I will do this on my own time. I will work closely with recruiting. Please let me do this." Her passion was palpable, so I gave her the approval.

Ellen led an enormously successful effort. That year she received the employee-of-the-year award for this initiative.

DIRECTION VERSUS PRECISION

+ +

Most management meetings involve the presentation of financial information. All newly proposed initiatives include the related business case. The discussion of any problem is always accompanied by the financial implications.

Financial projections involve many assumptions and estimates, yet they are often presented with an unrealitic degreee of precision. Instead of a $2 million estimate, for example, overeager planners might present decision makers with a figure of $1,995,086—and sometimes they even include the cents.

Things get even worse when people in a meeting start to debate and discuss the numbers at the same level of specificity. Someone might say, "I'm not sure we will achieve a 10 percent growth rate. It may be closer to 9.5 percent."

When numbers appear in a presentation to assist in the discussion of a problem, too often people focus on the numbers and ignore the real issues.

If everyone in a meeting accepted the fact that numerical projections were useful for indicating the direction and overall size of an opportunity or problem and were not intended to be precise forecasts, discussions would focus more on the opportunity or problem.

Once I was presenting to an executive team on a bet-the-farm issue. Our analysis showed that if they did not handle the problem properly, they stood to lose as much as half of their revenue stream within the year. Clearly, it was a very serious situation. For a few minutes, the conversation was all about the numbers—assumptions and estimates—and tweaking the analysis. There was no discussion of the problem. It was as if the purpose of the meeting was to evaluate the financial model.

Finally, I stepped in and said, "Thanks for all your comments on the model. They were very helpful. We have sent the model to each of you, so when you get back to your office, feel free to suggest adjustments.

"For now, let's assume our model is wrong. Instead of losing 50 percent of your revenue, you lose only 25 percent. Can we agree this is a big problem? Then let us discuss the actions we can take to stop, reduce, or slow down the revenue decline."

When using numerical models in the discussion of a business issue, it is important to agree on the assumptions in the model. But if the financial model is correct in its direction, avoid discussing the precision of the numbers and stay focused on the business issues instead.

INDUCTIVE REASONING

+ +

Recently, my friend Linda asked me for some assistance. Linda is the CEO of a small family-held business. She was considering purchasing a smaller competitor, River, Inc. She spent an hour going over the particulars of her company and the competitor.

She then asked, "Do you know someone who can value River?"

I replied, "Ray, a friend of mine, is an accredited valuation expert. He can probably do a quick and dirty valuation based only on the information that you have now."

Linda met with Ray and gave him the relevant information. A week later, I met Ray at the local coffee shop to review the draft of his valuation.

"Ray, before we start, I want you to know that I am going to use inductive reasoning." I actually said this because I wanted Ray to know where I was coming from.

"Okay," he replied, "but you have to tell me what 'inductive reasoning' means."

"Well, I met with Linda for an hour before she called you. Based on that discussion, I walked out with a working hypothesis that the value of the competitor is around $8.5 million."

Ray asked, "Did you have any additional information or do any analysis?"

"No. I just based it on our discussion and my general experience. It's like someone said, 'Based on what you know after an hour, if you had to bet the ranch on one value, what would it be?' And that number for me is $8.5 million. I am obviously open to the value being higher or lower based. But on the other hand, I would need to be *convinced* that the value is much higher or much lower."

I looked at Ray's valuation and noted that the range was $10 million to $13 million. At the midpoint, it was $3 million higher than my hypothesis.

"So, Ray, I am already biased against the value that you have arrived at."

I then started reviewing the analysis, looking for assumptions and methodology that would lead to a higher value than I thought.

I read through the entire valuation, making notes but not commenting. When I finished, I still thought the valuation was too high, and I was ready to ask detailed questions.

"Ray, I have the following comments and questions:

1. The public company multiple looks high. Are these companies really comparable to the target company? They are in better performing segments of the industry.

2. The EBITDA (earnings before interest, taxes, depreciation, and amortization) is from last year. Given the industry downturn, is the target company doing worse this year?
3. Should the public company multiple be discounted since the target company has only $8 million of revenues?
4. These comparable mergers and acquisition transactions are from the past four years when the construction industry was booming. Now that there is an industry downturn, should you discount the sales multiples?
5. In your weighted average cost of capital calculation you used a low cost of debt interest rate. At what rate could such a small business actually borrow?
6. In the asset values calculation, you include excess cash in the high side of the value. The seller would probably keep the excess cash."

Ray took all of my points and questions in a constructive way and commented, "I can't believe how quickly you went through that."

"That is the beauty of inductive reasoning. I was very focused on what I was looking for."

This process enables you to review the work of others in a much more time-efficient manner. It also enables you to be much more effective and insightful in your review because you are focused on the meaningful issues and not the trivial ones.

YOU CAN'T REVIEW
WHAT YOU DO

+ +

Ray said, "I can't believe you had all those comments. I should have caught some of those items."

"Not necessarily, Ray. It's very difficult to review original work that you have done yourself. You are focused on following the appropriate methodology and finishing on time.

"When you review your own work, it's in the context of the approach you use. It's very difficult to look at it differently. That's why, after a while, I stopped doing any original work. I knew that I wasn't good enough to do the work and then review it in a holistic manner.

"Furthermore, most valuations are all about the proper application of the methodology and not about whether or not the answer actually makes sense.

"If you start with the answer that makes sense and then do the valuation (inductive reasoning), you have a better process and then a better valuation."

I didn't expect Ray to be able to review his own work effectively. Therefore, when I reviewed his work, I was not frustrated, angry, or disappointed. I was just focused on my hypothesis and whether his analysis proved or disproved it.

Ray also didn't feel demoralized about all the comments because I didn't give them in a critical way. I gave the comments as a possibility—what if we looked at it this way?

Oh, by the way, Ray redid the valuation. The new range was $7.5 million to $9 million.

Don't expect people to do things the way you would do them or to be able to review their own work as well as you would. This will enable you to review the work of others more constructively than critically.

SUPPORT YOUR STAFF

+ +

While Rich, one of our new hires, was working on a financially troubled company, he pissed off every person he met. I think he even pissed off some people he hadn't met. I eventually had to call him into my office.

"Rich, I understand that you have pissed off every person at the client's company, as well as the rest of our team, in just two weeks. That was pretty quick. Let me tell you how you are going to fix this."

Rich immediately argued, "But Mike, you haven't heard my side of the story."

"Your side of the story is irrelevant. If you want to fix this, then you will do what I say."

"But, but, but . . ."

"No buts, Rich. You are going to apologize to every person you have met. You will tell them it is your fault that there was a disagreement and that you didn't mean to anger them."

Rich reluctantly agreed and went out to start apologizing. Minutes later the client's CEO, Ken, called me and asked me to stop by his office.

As soon as I stepped into Ken's office, he said, "We have a problem with Rich."

"Yes, I know. I have already spoken with him, and the problem is being fixed."

"Well, Mike, I want Rich taken off the assignment."

"Fine. Today will be Rich's last day."

"That was easy. I thought you were going to fight me on this."

"Not at all. I believe that clients should be able to decide who works on their matters. Do you have a piece of paper?"

Ken handed me a legal pad. "Why?"

"I'm going to write down the names of my competitors and their phone numbers."

"Why?"

"Oh, did I mention that if Rich goes, I go?"

A moment went by before Ken grudgingly replied, "Hmm, Rich can stay."

"Whatever you want, Ken."

Your staff will greatly appreciate public and private displays of support. Also, clients need to be managed in an artful, nonthreatening manner wherever possible.

HIRE ADULTS

+ +

I have always had little time or patience for petty issues, especially when people act childishly.

I treat people like adults. In turn, I insist they act like adults.

One afternoon during the first year of our firm's operation, Paul, an employee, came in to complain about some petty issue. Actually, I think he was whining.

I stopped Paul, whom I had known since college, and I asked, "Paul, how old are you?"

"I'm thirty-six."

"And you are married, right?" I knew this since I had gone to his wedding.

"Of course," Paul replied.

"And how many kids do you have?"

"You know I have four kids, Mike."

"Good. Then I have two words for you—grow up!"

Always require your employees to be accountable and responsible for their words and actions.

REMEMBER THE
GREATER GOOD

+ +

Aaron, a client of mine, sent me an e-mail a few years ago regarding a personnel situation he wanted to discuss.

"Mike, let me tell you the situation. Rex is a group head in our Sydney, Australia, office. He has been bad-mouthing the company leaders in Chicago and going around me on new matters. Rex is a bad cultural fit and is a negative influence on the junior people. I also think he has been interviewing with other companies.

"It gets worse. Right now he is away for the week dealing with the passing of his mother and the year-end holidays are less than a month away.

"I would like to let him go now. But with the death of his mother and the upcoming holidays, I am under pressure from others to delay it until January."

"Well," I responded, "this is obviously not a black-and-white situation. I learned something from Gail recently when she had to fire a number of senior managers. When I asked her how she dealt with it, she was remarkably matter-of-fact and said, 'I believed that my job was to take the company's situation into consideration. I put the best interest of the people who were staying at the company first.' So, Aaron, I think you need to put the needs and welfare of the people who work in Sydney first.

"Ask yourself, 'Will Rex's behavior negatively affect the staff over the next month?' Then speak with the most senior person in Sydney and ask the same question. If Rex's behavior is not negatively affecting the staff, then put his best interest first.

"But if you believe that Rex's behavior will cause harm to your personnel during the next month, then you should have him leave now.

"It's not your fault that his behavior is causing problems in Sydney. It's his fault. So, it is his fault that he has to leave now instead of after the holidays if he is likely to cause unacceptable harm to the people working at the firm."

Acting justly with the greater good in mind can often help when dealing with difficult personnel situations.

I KNEW WE SHOULDN'T
HAVE HIRED HIM

+ +

I was meeting with Nick, a young leader who is the head of a corporate finance group of a small investment bank. We were discussing the problems associated with the head of another unit at the bank.

"Gary is a real problem," Nick complained. "He doesn't fit the culture. He says he agrees on how to proceed, and then he does what he wants to do anyway. He is so painful to deal with. I knew we shouldn't have hired him."

"Whoa! What do you mean you knew he shouldn't have been hired?" I asked.

Nick replied, "Well, Mike, when the senior leaders of the firm met to discuss hiring Gary, I had a feeling that he wouldn't work out."

"Did you share that feeling with the rest of the group?"

"No, I didn't. It was just a feeling."

"Nick, let me tell you something. Every time I have made a mistake, my head—my brain—outweighed my gut, my intuition. There was that little voice in my head chattering away incessantly. And there was that bad feeling in the pit of my stomach.

"I bet you had all the reasons and rationalizations about why the decision was the right one. He had the right qualifications, the right experience, and the right contacts. And of course, no one else in the meeting questioned hiring him. Right?"

Nick replied, "That's exactly right. I went along with the group even though it still didn't feel good."

"Here's what happens, Nick. Maybe you don't know why it doesn't feel good. Maybe you share this feeling with others. Maybe you don't.

"Then sometime in the future, the naked light of day shines on the decision. Sure enough, the decision was wrong. And you knew it. You always knew it. Maybe you could explain why you knew and maybe you couldn't, but you still knew it."

Nick just muttered.

"Well, look at the good news. You learned a valuable lesson early on in your career. Your intuition is very strong. Listen to it. It is invariably right. Don't give in to the rationalizations and the reasons from the head."

IT'S NOT ABOUT
THE REASONS

+ +

A good friend of mine whom I advise asked me to be the temporary chief operating officer of his company until I found a replacement. He told me to think about it and let him know the next time we got together.

That night I tossed and turned while sleeping. I didn't want to do this job. I started rationalizing why I should do it: it was an exciting company, great people worked at the company, I was still young, and I would have new experiences. Though I wouldn't be able to play golf every day, five days out of seven would be enough. Still, it didn't feel good. A week later I met with my friend.

"So," he asked, "what do you think? COO?"

"No," I replied.

"Why?" he asked.

"A wise man once told me, 'It is not about the reasons.' Reasons are just explanations for what we want or don't want. So, no reasons."

He replied, "But if you don't give me reasons, then I can't argue with you."

"Yes, that I know."

THE SLEEP-AT-NIGHT FACTOR

+ +

Not sleeping at night? Is that your gut speaking? Have you gone down a path that you know is not right? Did you say something or do something that has left you exposed?

If you answered yes, clean it up right away. Keep a pad next to your bed. When you wake up thinking about the things that are bothering you, write them down. That way you don't have to worry about forgetting them. Then, go back to sleep.

When you start the next day, transfer the scribbles to something you can actually read. Then plan to address each of the matters on the list so they don't get you again that night.

When faced with decisions, pay attention to what feels right and what feels wrong. If it feels wrong, it will bother you at night.

Ask yourself when deliberating, "Will I sleep better or worse if I go down that path?"

Ask your people the same thing when they are deliberating about their own problems.

FIRE NOW OR PAY LATER

+ +

I have never heard anyone say, "I fired that employee too soon."

However, I could not count the number of times I have heard, "I kept that employee too long and should have fired him sooner."

I recently ran into someone whom I had not seen for six months. When we last spoke, he had been trying to decide whether he should fire an employee. "Arthur, how are you? Are you still struggling with that one guy on your staff? What did you end up doing?"

"I fired him last week."

"I know you were concerned about the rest of your staff. How did they react?"

Arthur said, "Well, remember I told you that he had a bad attitude with me but that his staff seemed to be supportive of him?"

"Yes."

"I was wrong. They all told me he had a bad attitude with them as well. Today, I was going over his area with his replacement and his team and realized that his work quality was really poor. His area was not well managed, and the bad attitude he had demonstrated with me had affected his entire group. During the time I gave him to try to improve, he just became more disruptive with his peers. We are all paying the price now to rebuild this area."

I asked, "Did you see signs of all of this during the last few months?"

"Yes, but I thought I was doing the right thing to give him more time to improve. Gail, I remember you saying that people always wait too long to make these decisions. Well, guess what? I waited too long."

I have never met anyone who likes to fire people. However, along with hiring and promotions—which are much more fun—firing is part of the job. Certainly, you want to be a fair and reasonable leader. This requires frequent, timely, and direct feedback so the person has the opportunity to improve. But if these actions fail, you are the leader and you get paid to make the tough calls. I also believe that we often know in our gut when we have to let someone go, but we try to override our instincts with logic and a desire to be nice (and liked). Do it and move on.

OXYMORON:
THE EXECUTIVE TEAM

+ +

In my experience, most leadership teams are not *really* teams. They are just made up of people who happen to report to the same person.

Using the analogy of a sports team, imagine what would happen if we got ten people together and declared the group a team. Afterward, however, we did not tell them what sport to play, how to win, how to keep score, or what position each of them was playing. How successful would they be?

But this is almost exactly what many companies do with their leadership teams. It takes work to create a team.

First, the team leader has to communicate to the team members their common goals and their individual roles on the team. Beyond that, the leader has to create the relationships and trust that are required for top team performance.

After the leader sets the right environment, he or she also needs to foster the right behavior.

At the offices of one of my clients, I was talking with the CEO about the dysfunctional nature of his leadership team. After I suggested that maybe he was not setting the right environment and tone for the group, he invited me to attend one of his meetings.

Early in the meeting, the CEO made a statement about the business and Tom, one of his business unit leaders, said he did not agree with the CEO. Before the CEO could respond, another business unit leader said, "I agree with Tom."

The CEO became furious and said, "Stay out of this. It has nothing to do with your business unit."

Another one of the business unit leaders piped up with, "But I also agree with Tom and Henry."

Instead of allowing this discussion to continue and fostering support and agreement among the different business unit leaders, the CEO became really annoyed that they were not supporting his view. He also got angry that they were commenting on one another's businesses.

The CEO said, "You should each mind your own business, run your own business units, and not butt into someone else's group."

At this point, Tom, who ran the largest business unit and was the first person to disagree with the CEO, was really angry and replied, "Then why did we all even bother coming here? If we are just supposed to mind our own business, we don't even need leadership meetings."

The CEO's last words on this topic to Tom were, "Shut up."

No wonder this was a dysfunctional team. The environment set by the CEO was hostile and did not foster teamwork or even group discussion.

The good news is that the CEO was surprisingly open to one-on-one feedback and coaching. We worked on his behavior, and he made significant improvement in his approach.

Creating teams is one of a leader's most important jobs. Teams are not created by issuing an organization chart and calling them a team. The leader must create, coach, and nurture a team.

KEEPERS, MAYBES, AND CASUALTIES

+ +

At one point in my career, I was asked to take over an under-performing business unit. I met with each of the people who reported to the guy I replaced. They were an angry, nasty group of people. They were not a team. They would stab one another in the back the first chance they got.

When I met with each of the leaders to discuss their business and what improvements could be made, all they wanted to discuss was how their peers were not pulling their weight. They were focused on internal bickering and politics instead of growing the business and improving profitability.

In order to assess the members of the leadership team as individuals, I reviewed their performance evaluations for the last few years, read their 360-degree feedback forms, reviewed client satisfaction rankings and trends, analyzed the last few years of financial results for their groups, and met with clients and employees from each of their businesses.

I met with them individually, to assess each person's ability to be a good team member, and as a group, to assess the team dynamics. I also listened carefully for clues from peers and their employees.

I then quickly put them into three buckets: (1) the keepers—high performers who could clearly work on a team; (2) the maybes—those who could become high performers and could work on a team; and (3) the casualties—those who could not improve their performance and could not work on a team.

I fired the casualties quickly but compassionately. Then I gave the remaining team members their performance metrics, 70 percent based on the team's results and 30 percent on their personal results. We then reviewed the individual segment plans as a team and identified areas of weakness.

Everyone was great at pointing out the weaknesses of the other plans. Then I asked them to help fix some of those weaknesses.

Every time they came to me to talk about someone else on the team, I asked, "Did you discuss this with the other person before coming to me with it?" Eventually, they stopped coming to me and instead worked it out among themselves.

They got the message quickly: collaboration was critical for the team's success. They could not win alone. They could win only as a team.

We celebrated team and individual achievements as a group. We worked on team failures together openly as a team. Much later, when we were functioning better as a team, we worked on individual failures in a team forum.

When someone suggested breaking the group up into smaller teams, which would have involved promotions for some of the team members, everyone said they preferred staying together as one group.

They explained that they were a team. The team had a turnaround plan that they were executing, and although progress had been made, there was much the team still needed to accomplish before achieving its goal.

We had become a team.

BEWARE THE BULLY!

+ +

We were once hired by a construction company to develop and roll out a total quality management program. The company needed the program to be in compliance with one of its large customer's requirements.

The company hired us after a very formal, structured, lengthy, and expensive proposal process. It had a selection committee that was empowered to make the hiring decision.

The first time we met the CEO was at a meeting to kick off the program with him and his executive team. Instead of letting us follow the meeting agenda, he began with a barrage of questions: "How many years has each of you spent in the construction business? Why should we take advice from you? What are your credentials? Why should we pay this outrageous fee? What can you possibly teach us?"

My team was trying to be professional and attempted to answer each of his questions and get back to the original agenda for the meeting.

Finally, I reached my limit with his bullying. But I knew that if I backed a bully into a corner in front of his team, he would only get worse.

I said, "Excuse me, but didn't you establish a selection committee, led by John here, to choose the consultant?"

"Yes, I did."

"Did you give them the authority to make the selection?"

"Yes."

I said, "Then please accept my apology. I should allow you and your team to spend time without us in the room. We will come back after you have had enough time to confer without us."

I then stood and started to pack my things.

He asked, "What are you doing? Where are you going?"

"We made an error. I forgot how busy you are. We should give you time for your team to provide you with the answers to all your questions."

He said, "But I want answers. You have not answered one of my questions to my satisfaction."

I said, "I know. And as I said, I am sorry. We gave all those answers to your team during the proposal process. We will leave so they can update you."

There was silence in the room as my stunned team and I packed up.

John began to whisper to the CEO, who quickly asked, "Wait, are you leaving?"

I answered, "Yes, sir. We do not want to waste your time."

"Lady, you have spunk. I will give you that. My guys tell me you have already jumped through all their hoops and answered all their questions. Let's get started." We sat back down and followed our original agenda. John told me after the meeting that the CEO liked to push people to see how they would respond. He liked to see whether they would knuckle under or push back. John continued, "When you started to leave I thought it was the end. I knew if you took him on in front of us that he would never back off. But all you did was apologize. Even though you were walking out and not taking his crap, you still let him save face."

Don't let a bully walk all over you. But don't back a bully into a corner since he will only get worse. If you let a bully know you won't knuckle under, but you give him a way out, he will usually take it.

Beware of the bully!

THE INTERN AND
THE HEAVY MANAGER

+ +

When I was a senior in college, I did an internship at one of the big accounting firms. On my first day, I was assigned to a client. When I arrived, I took out my shiny new briefcase (with nothing in it yet), smoothed out my new suit, put on my best smile, and walked in the door full of energy and excitement.

I extended my hand to the gentleman in charge of the audit and said, "Hi! I'm Gail Steinel, the intern, and I am here to work for you." He didn't shake my hand, which I eventually put back at my side.

Instead he said, "I'm Matthew, and I'm a heavy senior manager with no time for you, so don't talk to me. This is Alvin. He is the first-year guy. Don't talk to me, talk to him."

He didn't look too overweight to me, so I was a bit confused. All I could think of was the refrain "He ain't heavy; he's my manager!" I later learned that the term "heavy senior manager" was used for someone up for partner that year.

Matthew kept his word and did not speak to me for two weeks. During my internship with this client, I found something unusual and needed more information. Alvin told me another client of Matthew's had the same issue and maybe we could talk to that team. I asked him to talk to Matthew. But Matthew would not help us. So we were left with reinventing the wheel, researching the issue from scratch, and trying to come up with an answer on our own.

Though Matthew could have helped us solve our problem quickly, he was more interested in the seniority he had earned in the firm in terms of his title than in sharing that experience and position to help others be successful.

I did not accept a job from this firm after completing my internship. When pushed by staff from human resources for my reasons for not accepting, I told them about how Matthew was focused entirely on his own success. Later, I found out that the heavy manager did not make partner and had left the firm. Good for the firm! All people at all levels should be treated professionally and with respect.

LEADERSHIP RETURN ON INVESTMENT

+ +

One measure of a great leader is how many leaders he or she develops. This is as simple as return on investment.

Recently, I gave references to a potential new client. After checking references from past clients, past employees, and past colleagues, he called to give me some feedback. He said, "Gail, they said you were a leader who created a wake of other leaders behind you."

If it makes sense for companies to invest in developing other leaders, then investing in leaders who develop other leaders produces a multiple return on the original investment. But how do you identify these people? Following are a few guidelines:

- Look for the leader of the group who often cultivates other leaders for new initiatives.
- Look for the leader of the group who can fill an open leadership slot from within the group.
- Look for the leader who offers top talent for opportunities, not the one who hoards his or her talented people.

Leaders should create other leaders. If all you had to do was hire and fire, human resources could run the company. Leaders develop teams. They mentor and coach others. The best leaders help their team members become better than the team member thought was possible. It not only improves the caliber of talent when you invest in developing someone's skills but also facilitates the employees' loyalty to you.

THEY WON'T BUY BUNK

+ +

If we all hire highly qualified people, train them, and develop them to be even better, why do we assume they will buy all the bunk that is dished out to them? They do not buy it.

Say what you mean and mean what you say. If you try to pull the wool over your employees' eyes, they will not believe you, and you will lose their trust.

Most employees already know what is happening. When leaders don't acknowledge it, employees either think the leader is lying or, worse, that the leader doesn't know what is going on.

At one point, we were experiencing an unusually high turnover of our employees. Before addressing a large gathering of the employees in my group, I reviewed with my boss what I had planned to say. It was along the lines of the following:

- We all know that turnover has increased recently.
- We estimate the numbers to be about X percent.
- The exit interviews have identified three primary reasons, and these are the areas we plan to address.
- However, the majority of our employees are choosing to stay at the firm.
- In fact, let's celebrate and recognize anniversaries of long tenure. Did you know that X percent have been here ten years or more, Y percent have been here five years or more [etc.]?
- Each of you has made the decision to stay, at least for the time being. While I am sorry to see the others go, I am more interested in each of you.
- Please share with me now the reasons you are still here. Then let's make a list of the things you would like to see changed.
- Would you be willing to serve on a task force to determine the top three ideas for improvement?

After he had looked over the list, my boss said, "This is very good, but take out the first part about how high the turnover is right now. Let's not make them nervous."

I said, "Do you think they haven't noticed? Without the facts, most employees probably think the numbers are even higher." He let me go forward with my message.

The employee reaction was, "Thanks for being straight with us and sharing the facts. Your candidness was refreshing."

CONFRONT THE BRUTAL FACTS

+ +

Have you ever been in a meeting to discuss a problem and within a few minutes everyone has avoided the brutal facts, explained away the problem, and concluded that no changes are required?

Often, people don't like to face facts. That's because denial is a powerful urge. It allows people to avoid making changes. It also allows very smart and capable people to completely miss seeing some obvious things.

It is often helpful to have a third party involved in these situations.

For example, I once worked with a client that was losing market share. One day, I met with Rafael, the CEO, to discuss the matter.

"Rafael, have you noticed that every time your team meets to discuss this issue, they explain it away and take no action?"

"Yes, and then the next month we see the new numbers and realize that the results are just getting worse."

"Do you agree that the approach needs to change?"

"Certainly. Do you think we need more data?"

"No, you have all the information you need. The problem is no one has actually accepted the brutal facts."

Rafael asked, "What do you mean?"

"They are all smart, capable people," I replied. "If they accepted the fact that you are losing market share, they would realize that they needed to take some action. They are not accepting the basic facts."

"So how do we change this?" Rafael asked.

I answered, "In the next meeting, we need to force them to accept or challenge the basic facts. But we cannot let them delay the discussion by continually asking for more data."

The next meeting started down the same path until Rafael jumped in and said, "Okay, today there is only one question on the table. Do we all agree that we are losing market share?"

One by one, each person tried to challenge a specific data element or a specific assumption. But Rafael held his ground by replying, "No, that was not the question. There is only one question. Do you believe we are losing market share? What is your answer?"

Eventually, we got to it, and yes, they had to agree that market share was declining.

I asked, "Okay, now that we agree we are losing market share, let's hear ideas to reverse that trend."

Now everyone started sharing some creative solutions.

Rafael was very pleased with the outcome of the meeting. However, he was still surprised that it took so long for them to admit that they were losing market share. For him that point was obvious.

"Rafael," I explained, "the reason they were constantly debating the data and the assumptions is that they were avoiding confronting the brutal fact—they were losing market share."

Once they confronted the brutal facts, and only then, could they move forward and take action. Often, the underlying or root cause as to why leaders do not take decisive action is that they have not really confronted and *accepted* the brutal facts. They are hoping that if they continue to analyze data a new and easier-to-solve issue will come to the forefront.

HOW CAN WE SPIN THIS?

+ +

When you come across a mistake, or a perceived mistake, don't fall into the trap of moaning "This is going to look bad. What am I (or we) going to do? How are we going to spin this?"

This could be the first step down the wrong road. Your only comment should be, "It is what it is. Let's deal with it and then move on."

Spinning a story or trying to hide the mistake just adds to the mistake and is often worse than the mistake itself.

IT'S ALL ABOUT THEM

+ +

Once as a manager I presented to a group of first- and second-year consultants just beginning their careers at the firm. I introduced the material I had developed to present at a partners' meeting, which focused on the growth and profitability of the firm. When I concluded, my audience was silent.

"Are there any questions?" I asked.

One brave individual said, "While that was all interesting, what does it have to do with us? I came to this firm to get training, good experience, make money, and advance my career."

"Yes," said another, "can we discuss those issues?"

My presentation had missed the audience entirely. While you might feel passionate about a certain approach or message, if it isn't relevant to your audience, it isn't going to have much impact. Worse still, you will show yourself to be out of touch with your team, and very self-absorbed. But show them empathy, understanding, and insight in a way that inspires them, and they will be thrilled to be on your team.

Since that day I always remember, whether I am talking to an individual or a group, it is all about them—their needs and their expectations!

EASY ON THE SARCASM

+ +

I have a very sarcastic sense of humor. In your personal life and in one-on-one situations, sarcasm can be quite funny. However, in business you need to be very careful when using it. What you intend as funny can instead be embarrassing and de-motivating—especially if the recipient of your sarcasm is at a lower organizational level than you are.

When I was first promoted to the head of a unit, I was speaking to a group of junior analysts. I knew most of them personally and felt quite comfortable with them, so I fell into the trap of inappropriately using sarcasm. One of the analysts questioned my core message that we needed to hire more college grads and MBAs to build out the staff pyramid. He said that the "differentiator" that separated his group from competing firms was that his group had more experience.

Too aggressive in my response, I asked him for his average billing rate. He said that it was the same as that of other firms with a larger pyramid of less-experienced staff. And this is when I let my sarcastic side rip. I said, "Well, I'm glad you have a differentiator. Your differentiator is that you make less money than your competition. We have three choices: raise our prices, cut everyone's pay, or build out the pyramid. I choose build out the pyramid."

I immediately realized my error. I looked into the eyes of the individual who had spoken up and saw that I had embarrassed him. Later in this same discussion, I made sure to point out that he had been a member of the team that had just achieved a "go live" on a very complex project. He not only had brought the project in on time and on budget but also had delivered great customer satisfaction. I was able to undo some of the damage I'd done by being so sarcastic—but not all of it.

Over the years, I have learned to use sarcasm mainly in a self-deprecating manner. I make fun of how much I talk or I talk about my personal life—for example, how my mother complains that I am not ladylike enough. I have also learned to keep my temper and emotions in check. Sometimes a much less experienced person asks a sarcastic question in a public forum. While it is tempting to lash back and show such a person up, it is not the behavior of a leader.

DO YOU HAVE ANY ROOMS?

+ +

In the end, business and economics is all about supply and demand.

In 1990, the New York City hotel industry was beginning to slide into a dark period. Occupancy rates were falling quickly.

One night after working late in the city, I decided to stay the night in town rather than go home. I didn't have a hotel reservation, but I figured it would be easy enough to find a room.

I cruised down Madison Avenue and into the Omni Hotel. I walked up to the front desk and asked for a room.

"Yes sir," the desk clerk replied. "Would you like a standard room or a deluxe room?"

"A standard room would be fine, thanks."

"Yes, sir. The rate for a standard room is $249."

"Fine," I replied. "I am prepared to pay $125."

"But sir, the rate is $249."

"Yes, I know. But I am prepared to pay $125."

"Sir, I can't do that."

"That's okay. Is the night manager around?"

"I will get him, sir."

The night manager came out and said, "Good evening, sir. Can I help you?"

"Yes, I am looking for a room."

"I understand. Our standard rate is $249."

"I am willing to pay $125."

"$125?" asked the manager.

"Yes. It is 12:30 a.m. Most likely nobody else is coming in tonight. So, I figure $125 is better than not booking the room for the night, and I will be gone by 7:00 a.m."

The night manager said, "Fine. Give him the room for $125."

"Thank you. Would this be a bad time to ask for an upgrade?"

REPETITION, REPETITION, REPETITION

+ +

If you want your message to really be heard, you need to repeat it, repeat it, repeat it.

After performing an analysis of our client portfolio, I presented it to the leadership team. I said, "This four-quadrant matrix is our client portfolio. The horizontal axis is the size of the account and the vertical axis is the gross margin. The midpoint of the vertical axis is the break-even point."

John said, "Wow, the largest percentage of our clients is in the lower-left quadrant."

Mark added, "No wonder we don't make enough money."

The head of sales commented, "If this is gross margin, the results are even worse because this does not include SG&A [selling, general, and administrative] costs."

John added, "But changing this will take years. We need to make improvements now."

I said, "Actually, 25 percent of the contracts in the lower-left quadrant are due to be completed this month."

Mark said, "We should immediately determine that either the next project will be more profitable or stop selling work at those companies."

John said, "Then we can redeploy those resources to accounts in the upper-right quadrant."

Mark cautioned, "We do need to be careful. Some of these accounts can become accounts in the upper-right quadrant, and this is the investment period."

I replied, "Yes, but we need to establish a time period in which to achieve that status."

Someone said, "How about six months?"

I added, "Now we need a simple way to communicate this message."

The head of sales said, "How about, 'We are going to the upper right'?"

The term *upper-right* became shorthand for the change we would make over time in the client portfolio. We would begin to serve larger companies with large consulting budgets. We would focus on projects with higher profit margin potential.

We shared the four-quadrant matrix with the entire group, explaining the analysis and our goals.

We then started on the repetition path. The charts and our progress were sent out every month. Every week on our deal review calls we asked, "Is this an upper-right contract? Does this account have upper-right potential?"

Before I went to a client, I would ask the team, "Is this an upper-right account? If not, what is the plan to get there?"

For all lower-left accounts, we reviewed the status and progress every week to make sure we were reducing the number of accounts in that quadrant.

My team and I never met with employees without discussing the move to the upper right. No investment was made without addressing the potential to move us faster to the upper right.

When we began to make progress, we moved into even higher degrees of repetition.

We referred to the upper right on a daily basis for eighteen months. By then, it was just part of the entire group's vocabulary. We dramatically changed the portfolio mix.

Messages need to be simple and consistently delivered to have impact and be memorable. But even the best messages will not get through unless they are repeated over and over and over again.

but somehow we needed to be a part of the game that night. Listening to the game made things feel normal. Winning had also become the norm during our football seasons. The team was on a thirty-four game winning streak including two consecutive state championships. But this night, things were different. I wasn't there, and it felt strange, even under our circumstances. It appeared the team was also playing like something wasn't right. Even the radio announcers were making comments about the team's unusual lackluster performance. We were not playing on all cylinders. We were on the road and down late in the fourth quarter to an excellent football team. Our defense had played a tremendous game, giving us a chance to win. Our offense, however, was struggling to move the ball, and it appeared that the winning streak would come to an end. Then suddenly, we scored on a short pass that broke for the game-winning touchdown. Back at home, the cheers of joy coming from my bedroom were mixed with tears and hugs.

It is hard to describe the mix of emotions we were feeling, but somehow, I knew our tears represented the beginning of the healing process. This win was big for my family and me. Perhaps even bigger than the two previous state championship games we won. The Lord had used the coaches and players of Sandy Creek High School as His instruments to begin the healing process in our lives. A few days later, dressed in their red jerseys, the team came to Zack's memorial service, and I was able to hug the coaches and

2
Getting the Right View

One of my favorite movies is *Evan Almighty*. It is a great family-friendly movie with some powerful messages. The plot of the story is that God, played by Morgan Freeman, has chosen Evan Baxter, played by Steve Carell, to build a modern-day ark. When Evan responds to God that building an ark is really not part of his plans, God laughs. It's a classic movie scene that sheds light on the important truth that God's plans for our lives don't always match ours. Coaches are very strategic and careful when it comes to making plans. Sometimes, offensive coordinators even script out the first ten plays of a ball game. Planning involves anticipation, expectation, and most importantly, hope. At the beginning of our seasons, hopes are high as the plan is put into action. The reality of our profession, however, is that, sometimes, things don't go according to plan. What we anticipated happening doesn't happen. Our expectations for teams and ourselves are not met, and the high hopes we had are lost.

So, how do we respond? Our response to things we can't control is crucial, and it is closely tied to a key word: perspective. *Perspective* is the lens through which we view life. Simply put, it is how we look at things. Before we respond, we must have the proper

CREATING GOOD LUCK

+ +

My mother has always told me that one of the ways you can create what we often refer to as good luck is to be open to new experiences or opportunities.

They often turn out to be your lucky break.

One such experience happened to me on the day of my promotion to manager. The managing partner of the office called me in to his office and said, "Congratulations, Gail, on a well-deserved promotion to manager."

I thanked him, and he added, "I received this notice about a training school for cost-reduction consulting that the firm would like to build and grow. I would like you to attend."

"But I am an auditor and my promotion proves I am good at it. Why should I start to do something else?"

"You will still be an auditor. However, we are being asked to send some of our best performers. Just go and check it out."

So off I went to a one-week training program. I was not a happy camper, but I figured I would make the best of it. Much to my surprise, the training class was great.

I asked the instructor, "What is the firm's plan for building this business on a global basis?"

He responded, "I'm not sure. I was just asked to teach the class on this cost-improvement methodology."

I said, "But this is a great business. We should invest and build it globally."

I had the bug! I wanted to build a business. So much for being an auditor!

On the plane home, I wrote up a business plan that included a financial forecast. Monday morning I met with the managing partner and presented my plan.

He said, "This is great, but don't forget you still need to serve your audit clients. If you want, give it a shot."

The next day I was at my largest client and went out to lunch with the CEO and CFO. They were discussing some of their challenges. In particular they needed to lower their cost structure.

George, the CEO, said, "Yeah, I have a call set up with some guys from McKinsey when we get back from lunch. I am going to ask them for a proposal."

This was my moment.

I explained, "George, I just came back from a training session on cost-reduction consulting. We have a detailed methodology. We could do a great job."

George said, "But you have never done it before. I need this done right."

I replied, "Okay, so McKinsey has done cost-reduction work before and I've just gone to a training class. But I have been on your account for five years. I know your business inside and out. They know nothing about your company."

George said, "Well, that's true. You do know us."

I said, "I can also reach out to people in our firm who have done this before."

Then I added, "You know that no one will work harder than me on this for you."

I could tell he was at least considering it. However, my lack of experience was worrying him.

I told him that I had an idea, and I asked him to give me a month to do the overall assessment to identify the cost-savings opportunities. I assured him that if he was not happy with the work, he didn't have to pay us, and that he would still have time to hire another firm before the quarter ended.

He eventually gave us the project. It was a huge success for his company.

For me, it changed my career forever. I became one of the founding members of our consulting business.

Eventually, I became the global managing partner of a $2.5 billion consulting business.

That was clearly my lucky break. But I always wonder, was it luck or was it really my willingness to try something new?

If you focus on building your skills and your network; if you are willing to try new things—often lateral moves; if you stay inquisitive so you learn more; and if you are always open to new opportunities, you can often create good luck.

VACATION NONSENSE

+ +

We sold our firm one January, and as part of the deal I received quite a few weeks of vacation each year.

Just before Thanksgiving that year, I looked at my records and realized I had four weeks of vacation left. Never one to read the firm policies manual, I called our division president.

"El Presidente, how are you today?"

"Good morning, Mike. What's up?"

"I noticed that I have four weeks of vacation left. I was wondering what the company's policy is on carrying vacation over to the next year."

"Our policy is that you either use it or you lose it."

"Hmmm, can I carry mine over?"

"Mike, I just told you the policy. You can't carry days over to next year."

"So, if I don't take the vacation this year, I lose those days and I get no other compensation?"

"That's right."

"Okay, then I just want to let you know that starting today I am taking the rest of the year off."

"What do you mean?"

"Well, you just told me that if I don't take the vacation I lose it. And you said I don't get paid any extra for working. Therefore, I would be working for the rest of the year for free. So, I am going to take the rest of the year off."

There was a moment of silence before El Presidente spoke.

"You can carry the hours over to next year."

"Whatever you want, El Presidente."

It is usually better to make a reasonable request in such a situation than hang up and be bitter.

IT'S ABOUT THE CASH

+ +

Sometime after we sold our firm, the company put in a new billing system. There was a lag in getting the system online. As a result, there was a short period of time when the system couldn't generate bills to send to clients.

Todd, who worked for me, came to me and said, "The new billing system can't generate bills yet. What should we do?"

"Prepare the invoices manually, make copies of them, give them to our bookkeeper, and collect the cash."

Two days later I received a call from corporate.

Nick, the controller, said, "Mike, I hear you are sending out bills manually. We don't want anyone sending out bills manually. If you do that, we will have cash that can't be applied to invoices by the system."

"Nick, we work with bankrupt companies. They don't actually have a lot of cash. If I don't send the bills, we may not collect the cash.

"So, what do you want: cash with no invoices, or invoices with no cash?"

PUTTING THE INSTITUTION ABOVE THE SELF

+ +

Leaders are stewards for an organization or institution who must remember to always put the good of the institution above themselves. The benefits will accrue for both the institution and the individual.

One of my clients had the people with the right skills in his business unit to help another unit win a big contract. He assigned his team to help out, and they got the deal. But because they were separate units in separate lines of business, his unit didn't receive any credit. Not only did his team not get the credit, his own results suffered too because he lent his staff. But he knew it was the right thing to do for the company as a whole.

In that case, it all turned out for the best. At the end of the year the CEO gave him a discretionary bonus for doing the right thing even though it hurt his unit's financial results.

In my experience, people want to feel part of an institution that is bigger and more important than any one person. When leaders put the good of their organizations above their own careers, not only will they be doing the right thing, given their fiduciary responsibilities, but senior executives will also notice and reward them.

Your team will see this and trust you more with their careers as well.

JUST BRING IN
THE REVENUE

+ +

When I took the stage during a company meeting a few years ago, I knew my message had to be simple and clear, because the staff was upset that bonuses were not very good that year. When asked directly about the bonuses, I said, "All good things come from revenue. Your job is to bring in the revenue. My job is to run the business efficiently so enough of that revenue drops to the bottom line and is available for bonuses."

Someone then said, "We also need more training."

I responded, "All good things come from revenue—not just bonuses."

Someone said, "But what can we do about revenue? Isn't that management's job?"

"Yes," I replied, "but don't you want to be able to control your own destiny? Don't you want to be able to make sure there is adequate investment in your training and development? Don't you want money available for higher raises and bonuses?"

He responded, "But even if we could increase revenue, it would take too long. We need changes now."

"Did you know that in our business, on average it takes just four weeks to sell add-on work to an existing client and twelve weeks for a new client?"

Someone else added, "But we still have to wait until the end of the year for our bonuses."

"I will make you all a deal. Let's spend the rest of this session focusing on how we can increase revenue as quickly as possible. I will agree to make an exception this year and pay out bonuses on a quarterly basis."

The group was engaged. They understood two simple and clear messages: All good things come from revenue, and revenue is directly and immediately linked to employee bonuses.

When I came off the stage, one of the senior executives came up to me and said, "Gail, this is a smart group of people. Didn't they already know that the business needs revenue?"

I replied, "Yes, but it still needs to be said from time to time."

Many ideas came from the floor, most of which we implemented. That year, our revenue and profits grew dramatically, and we were recognized as the fastest-growing consulting firm.

All communications should be simple and clear.

LIVING YOUR VALUES

+ +

One time, the manager responsible for my largest client came to me with a sexual harassment issue. A member of our staff had been sexually harassed by one of the client's team members. When I asked the manager to tell me the details, she said, "I'm not really sure. Our team member doesn't want to make a big deal out of it."

"Well, this is a big deal," I said. "Ask her to come see me."

Our team member came to my office the next day and was quite upset. "Gail," she said, "they should never have told you about this. I know it's our biggest client, and I don't want to make trouble. Just forget it."

"Why don't you tell me what happened, and then we can determine what we should do about it."

When she was done, I told her that what had happened was a big deal and we would take immediate action.

The next day I met with the executive sponsor at the client. After sharing the background, I told him that we needed this individual removed from the project and officially reprimanded, or we would need to resign from the project.

The client was 100 percent supportive, and it was all done the next day.

At the next staff meeting, someone said, "That was great to see you stand up for us and do the right thing."

Living your values means doing it not only when it is convenient but also when it means making tough choices.

THAT'S LEADERSHIP?

+ +

Require your top people to speak and act like leaders. One day I saw one of my senior staff do something that I didn't think was very leader-like. So, I spoke with him about it afterward.

"Hi, Rick, how's it going?"

"It's going fine, Mike. What's up?"

"Rick, I happened to be walking by earlier today when I saw you go into the staff room. I then heard you yell at a young associate for asking someone to call you and not warning you that you would be getting a call."

"But Mike, I got this call and wound up spending an hour, which I didn't have, on the call, and I was pissed."

"Do you consider yourself a leader?"

"Yes, I do."

"Does yelling at a staff person in front of everyone else for not telling you a call was coming fit your definition of a leader?"

Rick sighed and replied, "No, it isn't what a leader should do."

"No, it isn't," I replied. "And, Rick, do you also realize that you tried to defend your action to me?"

"Hmmm, I guess so."

"Not very leader-like either, is it?"

"No."

"Rick, hold yourself to your standard of how a leader should speak and act. This will serve you well."

FINE WINE AND
THE BOTTOM LINE

+ +

A few years ago my buddy Jack took a couple of guys from the office out to dinner with Greg, an employee who wanted to transfer to Jack's office.

At dinner, Jack turned to Greg and asked, "Would you like some wine with dinner?"

"Sure, that would be great," Greg replied.

Jack said, "Good, why don't you pick the wine."

Greg called over the sommelier and ordered a bottle of wine. When that bottle was finished, he ordered another.

When the dinner had ended, the waiter gave the bill to Nathan, who worked with Jack.

Greg had just left to visit the men's room.

"Oh boy, wait till you see this, Jack," Nathan exclaimed.

Jack replied, "That bad?"

"Worse," Nathan said.

Jack looked at the bill and said, "It is a little high but it's okay."

Nathan smiled, "Look at the other side of the bill."

"What is this?" Jack asked.

"That's the wine bill."

"Oh my God! This is outrageous!" Jack cried.

"I guess we are lucky he only ordered two bottles."

Jack paid the bill, of course. Greg never joined the office.

The moral of the story: If it is on your tab, pick the wine yourself. Always keep an eye on the bottom line.

EXCUSE ME,
AREN'T YOU IN CHARGE?

+ +

Once when I was in Troy, Michigan, at a creditors meeting for a large retailer, I noticed the CEO hanging around outside the conference room shortly before the meeting started. Of course, I cruised over to speak with him.

"Hey, Bob. How's it going?"

"Good, Mike. How about you?"

"I am doing fine. So, another meeting . . ."

"Yes," Bob replied, "I really hate them."

I laughed, "Me, too. They are really bad. I think I *lost* knowledge at the last meeting."

He laughed. "Any ideas on how to make them go away?"

"No, but I have an idea on making them better."

"Oh, really? What is it?"

"Well, you have been the CEO of other public companies, right?"

"Yes, I have."

"At those other companies, did you let the outside attorneys run the meetings?"

"No, of course not."

"So, why do they run these meetings?"

"We are in bankruptcy."

I replied, "So? The attorneys work for you. Every meeting we have, the attorneys bore us with all the legal proceedings that are pending. By the time we get to the business issues, we are out of time and out of energy."

I continued, "It's even worse."

"How is that?" Bob asked.

"It's costing the company a lot money for the professionals to listen to all that."

"What should I do?"

"Run the meetings yourself and focus on the business operations. Let the attorneys for all sides meet separately and cover the legal issues. Then they can report back to their clients."

Sure enough, Bob took charge and ran every meeting thereafter.

If you're the leader, don't let the professionals be in charge.

THE LITHUANIAN BANK

+ +

Several years ago I was working with a domestic bank. They had opened an operation in Europe, and they needed a European banking license.

I went to a meeting of all of the bank's senior U.S. executives other than the CEO. Joann, who was in charge of special projects, gave a status report on the Lithuanian bank.

I had not heard of the need for a European banking license, and I had not heard about the Lithuanian bank before, so I asked, "Joann, who is actually in charge of the Lithuanian bank situation?"

After a moment of silence, Joann said many words. But none of them revealed the name of the person in charge.

I asked again, "But who is in charge of the Lithuanian bank? Who is the CEO responsible for the success of this process?"

Joann replied, "I have been asked to oversee the project to get the license, but I am not in charge of the Lithuanian bank."

"I don't understand who is in charge. Doesn't someone have to be in charge? Why isn't someone in Europe in charge of this? It seems as if someone like the person in charge of the European lending operation would be appropriate."

The executives had no answer. They indicated that they were each responsible for their functional piece of the Lithuanian bank, but none of them was in charge.

I pressed on. "Why doesn't the head of the European operations insist that someone in his office be the person in charge?"

I met with the CEO shortly thereafter. "Jeremy, I met with your executive team the other day. Joann raised the topic of the Lithuanian bank. There doesn't seem to be anyone in charge of the bank."

"No, Mike, we have it covered. Joann is in charge."

"No, Jeremy, Joann is *not* in charge. She is managing the licensing project. No one is admitting to being in charge of the bank."

"Don't worry. Everyone is in charge of their individual pieces."

"I have seen this movie before. If no one person is in charge of the overall situation, then it is highly likely to underperform, at best, and to fail, at worst."

"Mike, relax. It'll be fine."

I moved on to other matters. A year later, I heard the license had still not been received. I still didn't know if any one person was in charge.

If no one person is in charge of important initiatives, you are looking for trouble.

LEADERS USUALLY
HAVE FOLLOWERS

+ +

By definition, you cannot call yourself a leader if you do not have followers. Period. End of story.

Once, one of my direct reports came to me to discuss his frustration.

"Gail, my team just will not listen. They do not follow any of my instructions."

"They are not the problem."

Tim asked, "What do you mean?"

"If your team is not following, you need to look in the mirror and see why you are not making a compelling case."

Tim said, "But I am in charge."

"Yes, but you are not acting as the leader. A leader has followers. No one is following you."

We then went through the details of what he was communicating to his team and the manner of communication. We identified several areas that needed improvement.

Tim eventually made significant improvements, but he never became a great leader. He would always say, "But I'm in charge. They have to follow me." He never completely got it.

Once in a while take a look. Is your team volunteering to follow you? If not, you need to ask yourself why, and then come up with ideas that will encourage your team to follow you.

Leaders inspire others to follow. Leaders create opportunities. Leaders help others see those opportunities and take advantage of them. Leaders help others become better than they ever thought possible.

Any time you want to check on how well you are doing as a leader, turn around and see how many people are following you.

NOTHING IN IT FOR ME

+ +

David, a friend of mine, lost his job as controller when a new CEO was brought into his company. He called to ask me for assistance.

"Hi, Gail. I was wondering if you are aware of any openings for which I might be a fit," he said.

"Not off the top of my head," I said. "But let me look around."

After we hung up, I called a number of my contacts. About a week later I received a call back from Mary, one of my partners.

"If your friend is still looking for a position, my client has an opening."

"Great!" I said, and told her I could personally vouch for David.

He got the job of controller at a much larger company than where he had worked before. He was very successful at the company, receiving two major promotions within eighteen months.

To this day, many years later, this friend insists he owes me for that favor. I have repeated many times that all I did was pass on his resume, that it wasn't a big deal on my part.

"Maybe to you it was no big deal, but to me it was the difference between being unemployed and having a successful career," he said.

Although it didn't take much effort on my part, he never forgot it. Many years later this same friend was in a position to hire my firm as a consultant, and he did.

When you do something for someone, and there is nothing in it for you, that person will remember it forever. And if that person is ever in a position to help you, he or she will.

MORE CONSTRUCTIVE
CRITICISM—GEE, THANKS!

+ +

You know, I have never liked the term *constructive criticism.*
I always hear the criticism but not the constructive part.

So I coined a new phrase for performance reviews: "What's
next?"

Instead of saying "Here is what you did wrong and what
you can do to improve," I often say, "Now that we have
covered all the good things you did this year, let's move to
what's next for you. Here are the things we would like you
to work on in the coming year."

"What's next?" is much more positive and helpful than
constructive criticism.

ME READ? WHAT FOR?

+ +

At work one day, I was talking about a book I had read and how it had made me start thinking of things in a new way. Soon after, I ran into my colleague Phil, and I mentioned the book to him and asked him if he would like to borrow it.

"No, I never read books. I don't have the time."

"Seriously?"

"Absolutely. Look, I am already an expert in my field, and between the long hours and my family, I have no time for anything else."

Many years passed before I heard of Phil again. I spoke with someone who had recently run into him.

When I asked how Phil was, our mutual friend replied, "Actually, he's struggling a bit right now. His area of expertise is not in as much demand as it once was."

"I'm sorry to hear that," I said.

"Yes, well, as you know, he was never interested in learning anything new, so he suddenly found himself somewhat obsolete."

Great leaders are lifelong learners with an intellectual curiosity. They realize the value of learning, growing, and adding to their skill base.

PEER COACHING

+ +

While preparing for the performance reviews of my direct reports, I reviewed the 360-degree feedback forms for each of them. It was clear that the two of them were exact opposites.

One was a great P&L (profit and loss) manager and knew how to grow the business, but she needed improvement on the people side. The other was great with people and knew how to grow the business, but he needed improvement in the P&L management area.

They were both clearly keepers and worth the investment to help them improve in these areas. However, I did not have as much time available as this would require.

I remembered that they both were very good at accepting and acting on feedback, so I decided to try out an approach I had not previously used: peer coaching. I met with each of them.

"Sarah, it is clear from the feedback that you are a very strong P&L manager."

"Thanks, Gail. As we have discussed, this is something I am very proud about."

"Yes, but did you notice how low you scored in your ability to relate to your team? They seem to think you don't care about them."

"I did notice that, and it is consistent with feedback I have received in the past."

"Well, we need to make sure you do not receive this kind of feedback in the future. You are actually a great advocate for your team. What do you think you are doing that doesn't convey this to the team?"

"They want me to be what I am not."

I asked, "Do you want to be a leader? If so, then you need to make some changes, not them."

"But how do I improve in these areas?

"Sarah, I will certainly mentor and coach you in these areas, but I think we need to try something new. Would you be willing to work with one of your peers and do peer coaching?"

Sarah asked, "Can you explain what you mean?"

"I would like you and Marcus to work with one another. He is very strong in the people area, and I believe he can help you. I also think you can help him in the areas that he needs to improve. I would like both of you to enter into a commitment to each other to do peer coaching for one another."

"If Marcus is game, I will do it," Sarah replied.

Then I went off and had the same conversation with Marcus. They both agreed to give it a try.

I must admit I was not sure how well it would work, but it was a huge success. They both made significant improvements. I continued to meet with them one-on-one and together throughout this process, but I was able to spend less time then I would have if they had not done peer coaching. They both improved in several areas by working together.

During this process, I learned that coaching can be done quite effectively by your peers. Matching people with opposite strengths and weaknesses made both of them stronger performers. Most of all, I learned that this was only possible because each was truly interested in improving and respected the other.

IT IS ALWAYS PERSONAL

+ +

Years ago, I was involved in a proposal process for a very large contract. The client company followed a very structured and lengthy process, and we successfully jumped though every hoop.

The final major presentation to the entire executive team and all selection committee members went great. So we waited confidently for the notice that we had won the work. We waited and waited and waited.

We couldn't figure out what had gone wrong, so I called the executive sponsor for the client and we agreed to meet.

"Laurence, what is going on? We haven't heard anything. Have you decided to go with a different firm?"

"No."

"Is there more information you need?"

"No."

"Do you need to talk to more references?"

"No."

The conversation continued with similarly engaging dialogue for a while longer. It was like pulling teeth. Finally, I ran out of patience.

"Laurence, what the hell is the issue?"

After a long silence, he spoke in a very emotional tone and spat out in rapid succession, "Do you know how important this project is to the company? Do you know how visible this is? Do you know what will happen if it doesn't go well? Do you know what is on the line here?"

"Yes. But we discussed all of these points during the proposal process. What is hanging you up now?"

Long pause.

Laurence then leaned in and softly said, "Do you know that my job is on the line? I have never done this type of project before. What if it doesn't go well? I cannot afford to lose my job."

I was able to convince Laurence that we would do a great job for the company and that we would help him out as well. He finally put his faith in us, and we won the contract.

Although people think they make rational decisions in business, most decisions are affected by emotions. Decisions reflect on the decision maker as an individual as well as a manager.

If you can make a personal connection, you will be more likely to make a critical business connection. Remember: It is *always* personal.

MORE RISK?
MORE REWARD?

+ +

Shortly after we sold our firm to a public company, Jack, the CEO, called with an invitation.

"Mike, it's Jack. I have some good news for you."

"Great. What is it?"

"The board of directors has asked me to invite you to join the board."

"Well, that *is* great. I have two questions for you. First, will I be exposed to more risk as a director?"

"Yes, you would be subject to more risk."

"Would I receive more compensation?"

"No. You would not receive any more compensation."

"Well, in that case, no, I don't want to be a director. But thanks very much for the offer."

THE BUSINESS TRIP
FROM HELL

+ +

Many years ago a colleague and I went on our first business trip outside the country. Boy, it became a trip we will never forget!

We were working on a global cost-reduction project for a client. I needed to go to London for several days. I traded in my ticket for two discount tickets so that my colleague could take the trip with me. If you have ever traveled from New York to London in coach on a discount airline, you know that this trip did not start out on a great note, but wait till you hear how it ended.

After completing our work at the end of the week, we headed for the airport, using the London Underground since we could not afford a taxi. We were both carrying lots of luggage and briefcases. When we realized we were about to miss the next train to the airport, we began running. I slipped and fell, and I started screaming at the top of my lungs. My colleague Clint ran back to get me. I kept screaming that my ankle was broken. He was not initially very sympathetic. In fact, he was embarrassed by my screaming. After all, all I had done was slip and fall. I remember him telling me that I should just get up and run it off.

Someone came along with a chair and they all helped me sit down on it. I was still screaming, and Clint had become completely frustrated. I could tell by the look on his face, that he was wondering why he had been stuck traveling with a woman. Finally, he looked at my ankle. Within seconds, everything changed.

His face went white, and he started yelling that we needed an ambulance. I leaned over to look at my ankle to see why his attitude had changed so dramatically. But he yanked my skirt hem back down to cover it and said, "Don't look at it!" Now who was being overly dramatic?

I said, "Clint, don't be silly, let me see."

He became very serious and said, "Your ankle is turned 90 degrees in the wrong direction, and to top it all off your leg bone is sticking out of your leg!" I almost fainted when I heard his description.

When we got to the hospital, we were told that my injury was very serious. I had a complex break of my ankle and leg bones. It was a freak accident that occurred because the luggage I was carrying threw me off balance. I was told that I would need several surgeries and might never walk correctly again. To make matters worse, I was told that after the initial operation, I would not be able to fly for more than six months. After much discussion, I made the decision to fly back to New York for surgery and recuperation at home.

The decision to head back to New York for surgery meant putting my leg in a splint to enable me to travel without doing additional harm to my leg. Did I mention that I was still in excruciating pain?!

The doctor explained that I would need to fly in first class so my leg could be elevated for the entire trip. He also explained that even with my leg elevated, it would be a very painful trip.

What? Travel in first class? Remember, we were two people traveling at the cost of one! Clint had to call the office to get the authority to buy a first-class ticket. The company approved first class for me but not for Clint. Initially, they wanted him to travel on the discount carrier and not even be on my plane. Eventually, they agreed to let him fly on my plane, but in coach.

After hours in the emergency room, with the doctors making sure they did everything to hurt my leg even more, we were ready to head out. We took a taxi to the airport, where we were met by airport employees who had brought a wheelchair. At that time, wheelchairs had to be pushed by someone. Clint was the lucky person who got to push me around *and* carry our luggage.

We checked in at the airline desk and were told that the plane was delayed by two hours due to bad weather. The two-hour delay became a six-hour delay. Have I mentioned that I was in lots of pain? Clint took control of the bottle of pain pills since I was popping them like candy. He and I then began to argue and negotiate when I would be allowed to take another pain pill.

At one point, I had to go to the restroom. This posed a problem, of course, because Clint had to push the wheelchair, and he was not allowed into the ladies' room. We found a good samaritan who was willing to help me. She was great until we were coming out and she accidentally let the swinging door close right on my leg. I was suddenly in even more pain, and I began screaming again.

Finally, we got on the plane. Clint helped me settle into first class. When he sat in his seat in coach, he was the only one on the plane who was happy not to be in first class. For the next eight hours, at least, I was not his responsibility. He had passed me off to the flight attendant.

As we pushed back from the gate ten hours after I initially fell in the Underground, Clint breathed a sigh of relief— until he heard an announcement that we were headed back to the gate due to a passenger medical emergency. He told me years later that he was considering not letting anyone know that he was traveling with me. But it was not me. Unfortunately, another passenger was in distress. After an hour or so, we pushed away from the gate and were finally flying home. The trip seemed longer than usual as my leg swelled significantly during the flight. Did I mention that I was in lots of pain?

The story did not end for about a year—two surgeries, six months of being bedridden, two months in a wheelchair, one month on crutches, and three months of physical therapy.

We all know that business trips are not fun, but this was the business trip from hell. But as Clint learned, sometimes you have to take on more responsibility for your colleague than you had planned.

MORE VACATION NONSENSE

+ +

My buddy Dave started a new job on June 22. The company's vacation policy was that after six months, the employee received two weeks of vacation. The policy went on to state that no unused vacation could be carried over to the next year.

So, as of Saturday, December 22, Dave earned ten days of vacation. However, the company's policy gave the employees paid holidays for the 24th, 25th, and 31st, and the 29th and 30th were weekend days.

Therefore, Dave could take vacation only on the 26th, 27th, and 28th. He would lose seven vacation days that were not even possible to take!

Please, use common sense when creating company vacation policies.

BECAUSE THAT'S
WHAT HE WOULD DO

+ +

I once had a colleague accuse me of making a side deal to line my own pockets while working on a transaction. I was shocked and upset. I remember the conversation I had with my good friend, my coauthor on this book, who knew both of us very well.

"Mike, how can he say these things about me? I have worked for him for years. He knows my values and work ethics. How could he say this?"

Mike said, "People often accuse others of actions that they would commit themselves."

"What?"

Mike clarified, "Maybe he is accusing you because that is what he would do in your situation."

At the time I was blinded by my outrage. But as time went on I realized that Mike was right.

Since that experience I have paid close attention to what people say. I especially take note of the actions they accuse others of doing. This has helped me learn a lot more about their character and to project what they might be capable of, all of which has come in very handy.

DELEGATE,
DON'T ABDICATE

+ +

Once I called one of my direct reports about something in his area that had gone very wrong. "Kevin, how did this happen, and why didn't you tell me about it?" I asked him.

Kevin said, "I know. I am really pissed at Mary. I gave this responsibility to her and she really dropped the ball. I have her cell number if you want to call her."

"Kevin, does she report to me or do you?"

"I do, of course."

"Then why would I want to talk to her?"

Kevin said, "Because, Gail, she dropped the ball."

"No. You dropped the ball. You delegated but never followed up. She needed guidance and coaching to carry her responsibility through."

Kevin ignored me and said, "She really messed this up. You only know the half of it. Wait till I tell you the rest."

"Why did you give her this task in the first place?"

Kevin said, "She has always done great work in the past."

"Then don't you think you owe it to her to find out what happened here before you throw her under the bus in front of me?"

Kevin said, "I guess you are right. I just thought this was off my plate, and now here it is again and it's a mess!"

"You delegated it, but you can't abdicate responsibility."

Kevin never mastered this skill—and a few others. I finally ended up asking him to leave the company.

Delegation is a key skill of a good leader. But you can never delegate away the responsibilities that you have. The buck still stops with you. You are also responsible for developing and training the people who work for you and to whom you have delegated some work.

I THOUGHT IT WAS A
FURNITURE COMPANY

+ +

In the early nineties I was working for the creditors' committee of Seaman's Furniture Company. I didn't know the furniture business at all, so I was asking very basic questions.

I said to the CFO, "Go back to a period when Seaman's was profitable. How did the company make a profit?"

The CFO replied, "Sure, Mike. We were profitable when the deal was done with the private equity firm. Here is an analysis that was prepared at the time." The CFO handed me an analysis of the sources of profitability.

I quickly reviewed the analysis and replied, "Am I reading this right? When the company was profitable, virtually all of the profits were made by selling the receivables to finance companies."

"What do you mean, Mike?"

"Actually, for a number of years, your profits came from your financing activities, not from selling furniture."

The CFO grabbed the analysis back and looked at the numbers I had scribbled in the margin. "Well," the CFO replied, "I guess you could look at it that way."

"You have now witnessed the birth of an insight. Seaman's is not a furniture company. It is a finance company."

I shared this with the creditors' committee. The vendors on the committee were not buying the insight at all.

So, we showed them the analysis for the several years prior. Slowly but surely the committee members began to accept that Seaman's was a finance company, not a furniture company. As a result, the committee began to view the business differently.

It is always critical to specifically identify the sources of a company's profits, which may not be as apparent as one would think.

LET ME REPEAT
IT BACK TO YOU

+ +

Recently, I was speaking on the phone with a friend who founded a very successful company. He was describing a complex strategy that he believed would enable a bankrupt company's exit from Chapter 11. I advise him on certain matters from time to time, and he had asked me about his strategy.

"So, Mike, this is very complex and unique. Do you understand it?"

This is where you strike. Most people will say, "Yes" or "Could you repeat the part on the financing?"

Instead, I asked Ralph to let me repeat it back to him in my own words and then he could tell me what I missed.

"Sure, go ahead," Ralph replied.

I presented a detailed explanation of the strategy and its execution and told Ralph, "This should result in the maximization of your return."

Ralph replied, "Yes, that is pretty much it. Let me just emphasize a couple of the points."

This process served to accomplish two objectives. First, it confirmed to me that I understood the plan that Ralph had set forth. Second, it proved to Ralph that I understood him. This is a very effective and almost foolproof tool that I use often.

Ralph then went on to present another strategy, but he did it quickly. It was clear to me that this strategy was based upon some tax advice that he must have received from a tax expert even though he never mentioned the word *taxes* or referred to a tax expert.

Once again Ralph stopped and asked, "Mike, are you following me on this?"

"I don't know, Ralph. Let me repeat it back and then tell me if I am where you are on this issue." I told him my understanding of his structure of the deal. I then said, "Although you didn't mention it, I assume that the purpose of this strategy is to maximize the tax benefits of the transaction, and I assume that you received such advice from tax counsel."

I could hear Ralph smile on the phone, and he said, "Yep, you got it."

By repeating it back to Ralph this time, I was able to demonstrate a deep understanding of the strategies he was devising.

I couldn't do that by just answering, "Yes, I understand. Keep going."

When you are the one laying out the strategy, which approach would give you the most confidence that the person listening understands what you are saying?

1. Asking the person, "So do you understand?" and having the person answer, "Yes, I understand."

2. Saying, "Repeat it back to me so that I know that I said it right and you understand it," and having the person give you a detailed response.

FIRST THE RIGHT ANSWER

+ +

A wise audit partner to whom I reported during my first year of working taught me to do the research first, determine what I thought was the *right* answer, and then write it down. Writing it down while it was clear in my head and before it was clouded by conversations and groupthink was critical.

He said writing down all the relevant information I could remember was important because most issues in business are not actually black and white or clearly right or wrong. Most issues in business involve judgments, estimates, and assumptions.

He further explained that when the client has finished presenting their views and position on the issue, their arguments often sound compelling and right. At a minimum, they will seem close to right.

But if you go back to what you originally wrote down, before a persuasive argument was presented and you reached a compromise, you will be able to see how far you have moved from the *right* answer. This is particularly helpful when dealing with issues of fairness or equity or ethics. This approach has come in handy for me in many situations.

I have to admit that I have cheated on occasion and not written down my conclusions before getting the client's take on things. But if you do not write down your conclusion and logic, it will be easy over time to move further and further away from what you thought was right or at least the best course of action. So always, *always* write down what you think is right.

KNOW WHAT MOTIVATES
YOUR EMPLOYEES

+ +

When I was promoted to manager, a partner, Jason, called
me into his office.

"Gail, congratulations on your well-deserved promotion.
This is a key milestone in your career."

"Thanks, Jason. I am really excited."

He then said, "Well, you have a great future here."

"Thanks. I know it is years away, but I would like to be a
partner here some day."

So far, so good, right? Well, it went downhill fast from
there.

"Gail, you are the manager on one of our largest clients
and you are doing a great job. Your future looks great. As
a matter of fact, you can stay on that client until you make
partner. Then you can stay on it for seven years. You only

have to rotate off the client for one year. Then you can do seven years on and one year off until you retire. You have it made."

I sat there stunned.

I was only twenty-six years old. Why were we talking about my retirement?

To me it sounded like I was going to be doing the exact same thing for the rest of my life. I remember thinking, *They shoot horses, don't they? Maybe they could put me out of my misery.*

Misery? Wait a minute. A moment ago I was all excited about my promotion and great future. What happened?

What happened was that the partner was talking about what motivated him, not me.

You need to be aware of what motivates your employees. When you speak with them, make sure you address their motivations and not your own.

FINE WINES AGE WELL, PROBLEMS DO NOT

+ +

Recently, Martin, a member of my team, came to me with a major client problem.

"Gail, it looks like the estimates for this project were way off. At the rate we are going, this client's contract is going to be a financial disaster."

"Well, Martin, let's review the financials in detail with accounting and the contract terms with the lawyers."

Within one week of Martin's original call we met to discuss the decisions we had to make, and we came up with the following options:

Option 1: Wait. There were some assumptions in the calculations that could turn out more in our favor, and this might not turn out to be as bad as Martin had predicted.

Option 2: Take action immediately. Notify the client of the situation. Explain our error and the portion we thought was entirely our responsibility. There were three actions we identified to reduce costs elsewhere in the business to cover this loss.

"Martin, let's execute on Option 2 this afternoon."

"Don't you want to see more analysis?" he asked.

"Don't you think we have all the important facts? Do you think that analysis would add other viable options or change our conclusion?"

"Not really."

"Then why would we do more analysis?"

Martin said, "Shouldn't we take some time to think more about this?"

"What will change? Will we make a better decision?"

"No," Martin answered. "I think we have all the information we are going to be able to get."

I asked, "So why should we wait?"

He said, "I guess we shouldn't. It just seems quick."

"Martin, problems are not like fine wine. They do not get better with time."

Always take care of problems as soon as possible. Make the toughest calls first.

EASY ETHICS TEST

+ +

The best advice I ever received on ethics was from my mother. She said, "Gail, don't ever say or do anything that you would be embarrassed to read about on the front page of the newspaper." This has served me well over the years.

Here's an example of a time when I had to make a tough ethical decision. At my firm, if we paid tuition for an employee to get an MBA, that employee had to pay it back if he or she left within two years of receiving the degree.

One young woman left before her two years were up and didn't want to pay us back. It was clear we were going to have to go after her legally. Her father was a top executive at one of our biggest client accounts. The partner on that account asked me to forgive the debt to make her father even more loyal.

I gave the matter a great deal of thought. I understood it would make life a great deal easier for me if I went along with that scheme. But I remembered my mother's advice and did not. We pursued her and received the tuition refund. Her father remained a valued client of the firm. It was the right thing to do.

HOW COME YOU
DON'T SMILE?

+ +

I was advising a group a few years ago on various internal management items, and one of the managers, Bruce, wasn't so sure why he was meeting with me.

"Mike, how will you measure whether you are successful?"

"That's easy," I replied. "Every day I add value; therefore, I am successful."

I am sure he didn't buy that. A week later we met again. At the end of the meeting, I said, "Bruce, how come you don't smile?"

"What do you mean? I smile."

"No, you don't. I watch you walk around here and you don't smile. I have a homework assignment for you. Where do you live?" I asked.

"I live in New York City in an apartment."

"Are you married?"

"Yes," Bruce answered. "We have two kids."

"Good, here is your homework assignment. When you get to your front door tonight, I want you to stop and put a big smile on your face. Then open your door. I guarantee you that your wife will comment on your smile."

"All right, I will do it."

The next day I saw Bruce walk toward me in the hall, smiling away.

He immediately said, "Okay, you were right. You *are* successful at adding value."

"Why is that?" I asked.

"When I went home, I stopped and put a smile on my face before I opened the door, like you said. I walked in, and my wife said, 'You're smiling. You haven't smiled in two months.' I couldn't believe it."

One can add value in many ways, large and small, conventional and nonconventional.

GEORGE, ABOUT
THE COPIER . . .

+ +

One morning over breakfast with Mark and our friend Tara, Tara reminded me of a story about one of our previous bosses, George. George was not big on capital expenditures. In fact, George encouraged us to accept free legal pads from law firms—but that is another story.

One day I walked into George's office to tell him that we needed to get a new copier

"What's wrong with the one we have?"

"Well, for one thing, George, it's really slow."

"I don't think it's slow. And new copiers are expensive!"

For the next few weeks, we labored with the world's slowest copier. Then one night, at 2:00 a.m., when we were trying to get a report out, George went into the copy room to use the copier. Three minutes and twelve copied pages later, George screamed, "Why is this *?@! copier so slow?"

Two weeks later the new copier showed up. Your people work hard; give them the best tools possible.

THE THREE BIGGEST RISKS

+ +

When I was working with financially troubled companies, I was often asked to evaluate current CEOs. When I interviewed the CEOs, I always asked one question that invariably stumped them. Recently, I had a chance to ask a CEO of a financial services firm that one question.

"So, Hugh, what are the three biggest risks in your business?"

"What kind of risks are you speaking about, Mike?"

"The three biggest risks. The ones that would keep you up at night."

Hugh replied, "Do you mean operating risks or investment risks?"

"Just the three biggest risks in your business."

After a long pause, Hugh replied, "I haven't looked at our risks that way."

"Okay, here is what you should consider doing. Identify the three biggest risks to your business. Then assign one of your direct reports the responsibility of setting up a simple and concise reporting system to evaluate and monitor each of those three risks.

"The second step is to ask each of your direct reports to identify the three biggest risks in their areas of responsibility. They too should set up a system to evaluate and monitor each of those risks. Then ask each of your direct reports to require the same information from their direct reports.

"Think of how much better you will sleep, Hugh, when you have your five direct reports on top of the three biggest risks in each of their groups—and how much better they will sleep when their people do the same thing."

This is a very effective and efficient way to make sure your company or group is on top of the biggest risks.

ASK ME ANYTHING

+ +

Junior leaders should be encouraged to ask as many questions as they can. Once they start asking, resist the temptation to judge.

Don is the son of a friend who got a job at an investment firm. A few days ago he called me to say he was having a problem at work. So I asked him what the problem was.

"Well, people tell me to make sure I ask them questions when I don't understand something," he said. "But when I do, they make me feel like I shouldn't have bothered them by asking.

"Just the other day, I didn't know the right format for doing a spreadsheet analysis after meeting a client for the first time. But when I told my manager about it, he just got mad and told me I should be able to figure it out myself."

"Don, if someone suggests you ask them questions when you don't understand something, and then you ask and they are annoyed that you asked, find a way to remind them that they requested that you ask questions when you needed help. If the person's answer makes you feel small, tell the person how you feel.

"This will give them an opportunity to react positively. If that doesn't work, limit your damages. Wait for another time before approaching them again. Sometimes people are under pressure, which causes them to behave in a less-than-stellar manner."

"In the meantime," I added, "don't stop asking questions."

QUESTIONS, NOT ANSWERS

+ +

Many people think it's all about the answers, but you can add just as much value with questions.

I was working with an executive, Jerry, who was the head of a U.S. company's London office. He had inherited two senior executives who reported to him and to the U.S. headquarters functional heads. Neither of these two senior executives believed that Jerry had anything to add. As a result, they basically ignored him.

Jerry was pretty upset about this. "These guys don't listen to me, and they don't involve me in what they do," he complained.

"Jerry, they are busy. You have operated as a facilitator for the past year, not as a leader. To establish yourself as a leader, you must add value. Since they are functional experts, this will be difficult but not impossible."

"What do I have to do?" he asked.

"You have to ask great questions."

"What do you mean?"

"Here is what you do. You tell them that the CEO has asked you to be aware of all significant deals. Ask them to run every deal over a certain size by you. Read each of the write-ups and come up with a half dozen questions focusing on key issues and risks that are not addressed or are not addressed adequately."

"This will work?" he asked.

"Absolutely. You see, if they can't answer the question right away, they will be happy that you asked. You will have saved them from not having the answer if their U.S. functional head asked that question. I guarantee that if you ask great questions, these two executives will run everything by you because you will be adding value."

Jerry never did learn to ask great questions. The executives ignored him. And, of course, he was replaced a year later.

Had Jerry just asked questions—good questions—he would have started a process that leads to insights. Insights allow you to simplify the matter at hand and then change how you see what you are looking at.

Get in the habit of asking good questions. Good questions just take some thought, and they often lead to valuable insights.

OFFSET YOUR WEAKNESSES

+ +

I was on my way to a complex client contract negotiations meeting with a colleague when she said, "Thanks for coming with me to this meeting. You were great in our strategy session."

"Joan, I need to tell you about one of my weaknesses."

She said, "What do you mean?"

"I get bored very easily."

"Gail, what does that have to do with this meeting?" she said as we walked across the lobby to the elevators.

"When I get bored, I will agree to split the difference just to end the meeting and move on to the next issue."

She stopped at the elevator bank and said, "But we need to hold firm on our position. They are master negotiators."

"I know. That is why I am sharing this."

She said, "You could have picked a better time."

"I know, but we need a plan," I said. "Let's come up with a code so you know when I am about to give in."

She said, "Okay. Then I can suggest a break so we can talk."

"When you hear me start to say, 'Okay, why don't we do this . . . ,' stop me and suggest we take a break."

Joan said, "Okay, but you are really good at diffusing the tension and getting the client to trust you."

I said, "And Joan, you are a pit bull and will never give in."

Together, we did a great job at the meeting.

Later, she told me that she learned that day not only from my strengths but also from my weakness. Compensate for your own weaknesses with the strengths of the people on your team.

SPEND MORE TIME WITH YOUR STARS THAN WITH YOUR DUDS

+ +

When I was working for John, one of the luminaries in the troubled company advisory world at the time, I always wanted to spend time with him because I would learn so much.

However, one day John hired Peter. Peter turned out to be a problem child. Things weren't working well for Peter, and soon John was spending more and more time with him and less time with me and the others.

After several weeks of this, I stopped by John's office and told him that he had been spending a lot of time with Peter and that it had become difficult to get time with him.

"Yes, Mike, I know," he replied. "You see, Peter is underperforming. I think that if I spend more time with him, I can get him to perform at a higher level."

John spent significant time with Peter over the next year. Peter improved marginally, but he was still underperforming. Peter left the firm shortly thereafter.

Then, Jim was hired. He came to the firm with many credentials and maybe even more baggage than Peter. Sure enough, John started to spend a large amount of his time with Jim, his next project.

We all watched John spend many hours trying to save Jim. And you know what happened? Jim couldn't be saved. He, too, left the firm.

I believe that people get caught in the trap John got caught in because they have good intentions to help people improve. It's an admirable trait. They just need to exercise good judgment as to how much time to spend with underperformers and how much to spend with the stars.

Does it really make sense to spend more time with your duds than with your stars?

INVEST IN TALENT, TEACH, AND TRUST

+ +

Recently, when I was leaving a job, I received several e-mails of congratulations and best wishes. In some of the e-mails, the writers also shared a memory or a lesson they had learned while we worked together.

One of the e-mails came with this story from someone who had worked for me a few years before.

He wrote, "I learned to get the right talent for the job, teach them what they did not know, and then trust them to make it happen."

He added that when he was selected for the position to start a new business line, he remembered what I said to him the day we gave him the news. "Congratulations, Charlie. We have selected you for the position."

"Thanks. I will work really hard and promise to do a great job."

"I know you will work very hard. Your commitment and drive are some of the characteristics that make you right for this role. You also have all the technical skills that the job will require. But Charlie, there are areas in which you need to continue to develop. I will work with you closely until you build more experience."

He wrote in the e-mail that much to his surprise, we really did spend time together on the areas in which he did not have experience.

Then he wrote, "But the moment that I most remember was the day I came to ask your opinion and you said that I had enough experience and you trusted my judgment. I was even more driven because I wanted to earn that trust.

"You had invested in teaching me. Then you invested even more by trusting in me." The business he started was a great success.

We often become overwhelmed with time spent on our underperforming employees. However, the time spent that will pay the highest return is the time spent with your most talented employees. Spend the time to get the best talent into the right positions. Invest in talent by teaching and developing them. Then trust them to make the best decisions.

CELEBRATE SUCCESS

+ +

Most managers criticize early and often. But celebrate a success? Unheard of! I used to attend the worst staff meetings at one of the firms where I worked.

A co-head of the firm (I won't say "leader" since he was no leader) ran the most negative staff meetings. I dreaded attending them.

He always harped on what was not done correctly. Worse, it was usually administrative items like time sheets and expense reports.

Never ever could he say something positive and encouraging. Celebrate a success? He couldn't even admit to a success.

Celebrate success! People will welcome the recognition. The esprit de corps will rise significantly. And ironically, people will receive constructive comments much more readily when they are balanced with well-earned praise.

LISTEN, REALLY LISTEN

+ +

Once we were having an event that was sponsored by a software company. One of the company's executives got up to give a talk, but he was not a skilled public speaker. He spoke in a low monotone, went on too long, and was just plain boring.

I was concerned when the side conversations in the large room began to get louder. This was neither a professional nor a polite way to treat an invited guest. When he was finished, I stood and said, "Joe, I would like to thank you and your company for your support of our business.

"As I listened to your speech, I took away three primary messages for our business." Then I listed them.

A month later, I was attending the staff meeting of one of my direct reports. He ended by summarizing the key messages. After the meeting, I made a point of telling him how well he had run the meeting and that his summary was succinct and accurate.

He said, "Gail, I learned to do that when the vendor spoke at your last meeting. I was in the audience when you stood up and summarized his speech. Although he was not a very captivating speaker, you had listened to everything he had said, and when you summarized it, it had impact. You demonstrated to everyone in the room that you had listened to him, and you assisted him by summarizing his key points. I've tried to emulate that behavior ever since that day."

As a leader it is really important to listen carefully to the speaker and the audience. You need to hear the spoken and unspoken word in order to demonstrate leadership.

PEOPLE SPEAK THE
WAY THEY THINK

+ +

If you want to know how your people think, listen carefully to how they speak. People generally speak the way they think.

Steve, a CEO whom I advise from time to time, asked me to meet with Tom, who was in charge of a new investment initiative. The CEO wanted my objective views on the initiative to make sure it was being structured in a way that maximized the likelihood of success. A few days after our meeting, I stopped by Tom's office to see how things were going.

"Things are going well, Mike," he said. "What can I do for you?"

"Steve wanted you to explain the new initiative to me."

"No problem. Where would you like me to start?"

"It would be helpful if you could give me a sound bite that I could repeat to someone else."

Now, when I ask for a sound bite, I'm looking for something quick and concise.

Tom started a monologue. "We are interested in . . ." Tom went on and on. He rambled. He meandered. His monologue was not in any logical order. By the end of it, I still didn't understand the first thing about the initiative.

When Steve asked me how my meeting with Tom had gone, I told him, "Actually, not so good. Tom was all over the place. He really can't explain his vision in a cogent, concise manner."

"Yes, I know," Steve said, exasperated. "I don't know what I am going to do about it."

If people can't explain concisely what they are doing, they are unlikely to optimize results.

COMMUNICATION IS FOR THE AUDIENCE

+ +

Once when I was running a small group, I presented the strategic plan at a staff meeting. One of my direct reports was in my office waiting for me after the meeting. Robert said, "Gail, I have heard you explain this twice, and each time you drew the same picture. When will we receive the document to read?"

"What document?"

Robert said, "The document with all the details."

"But I presented it, and I drew the picture to help them visualize it."

Robert continued, "But we need a document that provides all the details."

"Why?"

"Many people like to read a document in private to reflect and absorb the strategy."

I said, "Robert, you have known me for years. Do you think I would ever write this document?"

He said, "That is why I am here: to convince you that we need it."

Now you need to understand that I am verbal and visual. On the Myers-Briggs Type Indicator, I am 100 percent an extrovert when it comes to learning styles. If it is going on in my head, it is coming out of my mouth—in real time.

But Robert was a strong performer. I realized that if he needed a document, others probably did as well.

"Robert, would you be willing to write the document?"

He said, "Sure. But I may need to spend time asking you questions so I can fill in the blanks."

I said, "No problem. Talking is what I do best."

Robert put together a great document that included the graphic I had been drawing each time I made that particular presentation.

Remember that you are communicating for the benefit of the audience, not yourself. There are many different learning styles in the world. Some people need to talk and listen, some need to read and reflect, and some need to see a graphic and visualize. If you want to communicate effectively, use all media and do not be afraid to ask for help.

GIVE UNDIVIDED ATTENTION

+ +

One of my clients taught me the value of giving your undivided attention. When I noticed that he was never interrupted by any calls or e-mails when we met, I thanked him and told him how I appreciated his undivided attention.

"Well, I am glad you appreciate it," replied Danny. "However, I do it primarily for cost reasons."

"What do you mean?"

"Gail, if we scheduled a one-hour meeting and I told you that you would sit in my office for an hour but we would talk only for fifteen minutes because I would be distracted by phone calls and visitors, what would you say?"

"I would suggest we just schedule fifteen minutes and then I could do other things."

"What if I told you that while we were meeting I would be reading my e-mail?"

"I guess I would say that I would just send you an e-mail that you could read."

He then said to me, "Since I do nothing else while I am meeting with someone, I do not set up as many meetings."

I then began to take notice that his entire team followed his lead. They all paid 100 percent attention during meetings and on conference calls. The result was fewer, shorter, and more productive meetings.

Shortly after I adopted Danny's way of holding meetings, one of my employees made an interesting observation.

"I have to be on top of my game when we meet. Since you give me your undivided attention, I have to be 100 percent prepared."

If you give 100 percent of your attention to people, they will feel great and will give you 100 percent of their effort.

THAT IS WHAT I SAID,
BUT . . .

As a leader, your words carry more weight then you realize. When you make a statement, recognize that it may be
repeated and misunderstood. In fact, one of the signs that
you are a leader who makes an impact is that people repeat
your comments.

I learned this while at lunch with a small group who had
all been my peers until I had earned a promotion. The day
after the lunch I was called in to the senior executive's office
and asked if I had said that I thought raises would be higher
this year than last year.

I said, "Yes, I did say that yesterday at lunch."

He said, "Gail, did you tell them that the company had
made this decision and will be announcing it soon?"

"No. Why would I say that? I have no idea what the company's plans are in this area."

He said, "Well that's the rumor going around the office. As I understand it, you just said that you thought the raises would be higher. You were just giving your opinion. Correct?"

"Yes."

"Well, they inferred that with your new position you now had access to confidential information. Therefore, they assumed it was not only your opinion but that the company had made that decision."

"Why would they assume that?"

He answered, "Since you were promoted, your words carry more weight than they did before."

Be mindful that as you progress in your career and take on positions of greater influence and access, your statements have more impact and your personal opinions can be misconstrued as the company's position.

AIMING AT THE WOODS

+ +

I have noticed that people are often reluctant to take constructive advice in work matters. In fact, people are often defensive in these situations.

I was once giving an employee, Bill, a review of an engagement on which we had worked. I was explaining how he could do some things differently on the next matter. He sat in my office with his arms folded, a sure sign that he wasn't happy with the conversation.

"Bill, you don't look happy about this discussion," I commented.

He replied, "Actually, I am not happy at all."

"That's pretty funny," I said.

He said, "I don't think it's funny, Mike."

"I think you will find it funny after I explain it. You and I play a lot of golf, right?"

Bill replied, "Yes, we play a lot of golf."

"And I am pretty bad, right?" I asked.

"Yes," he laughed, "you are pretty bad."

"So, when we are playing, and I say, 'Bill, you are aimed into the woods,' what do you do?"

Bill replied, "I say thanks."

"Even though I stink at golf you take the advice, right?"

"Yeah, so?"

"Well, I am an expert at troubled-company work, and I am telling you that you are aimed into the woods, yet you are not listening. That's pretty funny to me."

Bill laughed and said, "Well, when you put it like that, it is kind of funny."

Find any way you can to get your people to listen to suggestions for improvement.

WHAT IF IT DOESN'T WORK?

++

I often advised clients about a new course of action they were considering or the terms of a restructuring they were negotiating. There was often a lot of conversation regarding what would happen when the new venture or new deal was successful. Who would get what part of the upside?

At some point, before it was too late, I would ask a simple question.

"Excuse me, everyone. I don't want to rain on the party we are having here, but can I ask one question? What if it doesn't work?"

"Mike, come on. We have been over this. We believe this will work."

"I am not debating whether it will work or not. I am simply saying that it is possible that it may not work. Don't you agree it is possible it won't work?"

"Give us some reasons or examples of it not working."

"I am not saying it won't work, and I have no examples or reasons why it will not work. I am just saying, let's assume that it doesn't work for reasons we cannot foresee today.

"What would you do if this doesn't work out? What courses of action would you consider? What are the likely exit strategies if it doesn't work?

"What would you set up differently if you knew it might not work? Just think how helpful it might be to think of this now when you are setting things up."

Set up operations for success, but be mindful that they may not work.

SPILL THE BOTTLE

++

My wife and I were having lunch one summer day on the island of Malta. I reached for the olive oil and discovered, much to my surprise, that it was the brand that my friend Bill imports to the United States.

I picked up my ever-ready BlackBerry and e-mailed Bill.

"Hey, Bill, we are in Malta using the olive oil that you import."

Bill immediately e-mailed back. "Thanks! Every drop counts. But a true friend would spill the bottle."

NO ONE EVER EXPECTS THE SPANISH INQUISITION

+ +

In my second year at Arthur Andersen, I was working for a manager, Tom, on a bank audit. He had recently transferred from another office. One day while we were at the bank in a conference room, Tom was reviewing a file that I had prepared. Well into his review, he spoke out: "What is this? In the middle of your memo is the line, 'No one ever expects the Spanish Inquisition.' I can't believe you wrote this."

"Well, Tom, you are new here, and I want to make sure you read what I write."

"Well, I am glad I caught this," Tom replied.

"You mean you caught only one?"

If you make other people write for you, you had better read what they write.

WORK THE PROCESS

+ +

Too many years ago, I was working with Al for a bank group that had loans to a Chinese importer in the northeast, which were in default.

The company had hired Roy, a crisis manager, to assist in fixing its problems. Under Roy's direction, the company had prepared a new business plan that would serve as the basis for the restructuring of the company.

Al and I met with Roy to receive a draft of the business plan. Roy was proud that he had met the agreed-upon deadline for producing the plan. As Roy handed us the plan, I asked one simple question: "Roy, did you review this plan in detail?"

"I skimmed through the plan."

"You skimmed through it?"

"Yes, Mike. Is that a problem?"

"A business plan such as this requires a detailed review by you in order for the process to be complete. In the absence of such a review, I have no confidence that this plan was properly prepared."

Roy replied, "Mike, give me a break. I have a lot to do. It's fine."

"I will make you a bet. I bet that in less than an hour I can find enough material errors that you will conclude the plan has to be redone."

"You're on. I will bet you lunch that in an hour you will have found nothing material."

"Okay, Roy. Here we go." I turned to the balance sheet and said, "How were the amounts for inventory derived?"

I turned to the income statement and asked, "How did the company come up with the gross margin percentage, and how are they going to achieve that level?"

I turned back to the balance sheet and asked, "Finally, why don't accounts receivable amounts reconcile with the sales and cash receipts amounts?"

It took less than fifteen minutes. Roy couldn't answer any of the questions. Embarrassed, he took back our copies of the plan and said, "I guess I owe you lunch."

"Don't worry about it," I replied. "It wasn't fair. There was no way this group could produce a correct business plan the first time out."

On the way out, Al, who was relatively new at the time, asked, "How did you know the plan was wrong?"

"Al, it was a bad process. There was a low likelihood that the plan was right if it hadn't been reviewed in detail by Roy."

"But, how did you know what questions to ask to show him the plan was wrong?"

"Actually, that was easy. Those are pretty typical areas that companies miss the first time. So, I just started there. It was entertaining, though, wasn't it?"

TREAT YOUR FAMILY
AS YOUR NUMBER
ONE CUSTOMER

++

A number of years ago, I hopped on an Amtrak train in Newark on my way to a creditors' committee meeting in Philadelphia. At the next stop, Steve, one of the lawyers for a group represented by the committee, walked onto the train.

"Hey, Steve!" I called out, "how's it going?"

"I am doing well," Steve replied. "How about you?"

"Good, good. Come have a seat."

Steve then asked, "So, Mike, what time do you think this meeting will be over?"

"I think it will be over around 5:00 or 6:00 tonight."

"So what train are you taking home?" Steve asked.

I replied, "I'm taking the 2:40 home."

"The 2:40? I thought you said the meeting is going to end around 5:00 or 6:00?"

"That's right," I replied.

Steve, somewhat incredulous, asked, "Then why are you taking the 2:40?"

"I coach my son's baseball team, and we have a game tonight."

"But what about the meeting?" Steve exclaimed.

"Hey, nobody asked me if I was available for this meeting when it was set up. If they had asked, I would have told them that I had a commitment and that I was not available."

"But it is a Little League game and this is a committee meeting," Steve said.

"Steve, what if, instead of my son's game, I had a meeting with another client that was previously arranged. Would it be okay to tell the committee that I had to leave early?"

"Sure," replied Steve.

"All right, Steve, let me you ask you this. What is more important to you? Work or your family?"

"My family," replied Steve.

"So, Steve, why is it okay to leave early for another meeting but not for my son's game?"

"Well, Mike, when you put it like that, I guess you are right."

"No guessing about it. Always set up your family as a client or customer. Then treat them as you would treat your number one customer. You wouldn't cancel on your number one customer time and time again, would you? If you did, they wouldn't be your number one customer for long."

"Well, have you missed any of your son's baseball games?"

"Yes," I replied.

Steve lit up, "Aha! So, you missed a game due to work."

"No, I was away golfing with my buddies."

ABOUT THE AUTHORS

+ +

Gail is a twenty-nine-year veteran of the global management and technology consulting industry. She currently provides leadership development seminars, speeches, and executive coaching. A board member of Federal Realty Investment Trust and a frequent lecturer on leadership at Harvard Business School, Yale School of Management, and Villanova's Executive MBA programs, Gail is also regularly the keynote speaker and lecturer at BearingPoint's leadership program at Yale's School of Management. She is a CPA who has been recognized twice by *Consulting Magazine* as a Top 25 consultant.

Gail spent twenty-three years at Arthur Andersen. Her last position there was as the Global Managing Partner of the Business Consulting Group—with ten thousand employees in eighty-five countries. After the Enron crisis, most of her global team joined BearingPoint. She was an executive vice president at BearingPoint for five years, leading the Commercial Services and Solutions groups on a global basis. The Commercial Services group served clients in the energy, pharmaceutical, manufacturing, communications, and high-technology industries.

Mike spent twenty-five years providing restructuring advisory services regarding financially troubled companies to financial institutions such as JPMorgan Chase, Citibank, Goldman Sachs, MetLife, Bank of America, and Wachovia. He worked on hundreds of U.S. and European companies, from Arthur Andersen to Xerox.

At the beginning of his career, Mike spent seven years at Arthur Andersen, and then six years at Zolfo Cooper. In 1990, he cofounded Policano & Manzo, which was then sold to FTI Consulting in 2000. Since retiring in 2005, he has been advising the management team of Silver Point Capital, and he speaks frequently at professional firms and MBA programs, including Harvard Business School, London Business School, the University of Wisconsin, and the Yale School of Management. Mike holds a BS in accounting with honors from Villanova, where he is currently an adjunct professor in the MBA program. He is a CPA and a CIRA. Mike is also the author of *Wait, I Have a Story About That!* which is available at Amazon.com.

ACKNOWLEDGMENTS

+ +

Mike:
I would like to acknowledge a few people for their part in this production.

My parents, who did something to make me into a storyteller. My wife, Mary, and our son, Dave, who have always listened to my stories as if it were the first time they had heard them. Mark Fogel, who guided me through my first book so that this could be the second book. All my readers, including Mark, Tony Alvarez III, Steve Kass, and Dave Talesnick. Our endorsement friends, Andy, Bob, Don, Jeff, Paul, Tom, and Tony. Clint and his group at Greenleaf. And finally, my coauthor, Gail, who laughed at my unconventional thoughts and then went along with them.

Gail:

To my clients and colleagues who supported and inspired me throughout my career. Thankfully we also had fun along the way. A few of them who helped with feedback on the book include Camilla Sullivan, Terry Silva, Ira Entis, Sabina Henry, Jane Malhotra, Lisa Caldwell, and Miriam Hernandez Kakol. But most of all, thanks go to my family, who are the center of my life and my best friends.